Richmond Is for Children

4th Edition

Edited by
the Parents of the Sabot School

N
AMTRAK STATION
GREYHOUND STATION
UNIVERSITY OF RICHMOND
GAINES MILL
COLD HARBOR
GARTHRIGHT HOUSE
BEAVER DAM CREEK
CHICKAHOMINY BLUFFS
POUNCY TRACT RD.
SHADY GROVE RD.
NUCKOLS RD.
COX RD.
CHURCH RD.
PUMP RD.
BROAD ST.
SPRINGFIELD RD.
HUNGARY RD.
COURTNEY
MOUNTAIN RD.
WOODMAN RD.
PARHAM RD.
HERMITAGE RD.
GASKINS RD.
PEMBERTON RD.
THREE CHOPT RD.
SKIPWITH RD.
GLENSIDE DR.
HILLIARD RD.
LAKESIDE AVE.
GAYTON RD.
QUIOCCASIN RD.
FOREST AVE.
STAPLES MILL RD.
DUMBARTON RD.
PATTERSON AVE.
HORSEPEN RD.
MONUMENT AVE.
LIBBIE AVE.
GROVE AVE.
CARY ST.
WILTON RD.
RIVER RD.
MALVERN AVE.
WESTWOOD AVE.
BROOKLAND PKWY.
ROBIN-HOOD RD.
BOULEVARD
BROOK RD.
CHAMBERLAYNE AVE.
BROOKLAND PARK BLVD.
LABURNUM AVE.
AZALEA AVE.
SAUSILUTA DR.
WILKINSON
MEADOWBRIDGE RD.
ATLEE RD.
SHADY
POLE GREEN RD.
RICHFOOD RD.
LEADBETTER RD.
MECHANICSVILLE TPK.
COLD HARBOR RD.
CREIGHTON RD.
3RD AVE.

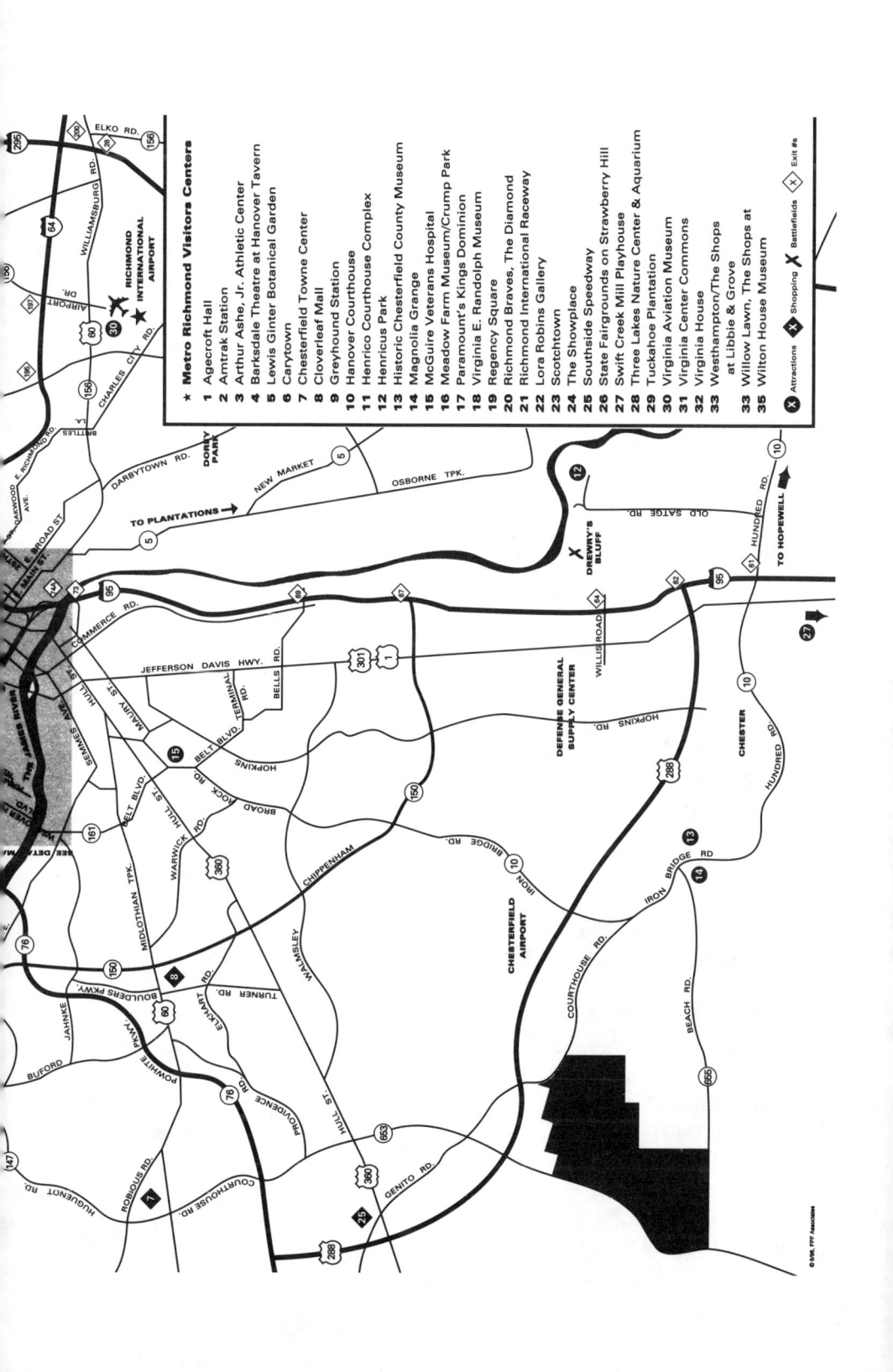

Metro Richmond Visitors Centers

- 1 Agecroft Hall
- 2 Amtrak Station
- 3 Arthur Ashe, Jr. Athletic Center
- 4 Barksdale Theatre at Hanover Tavern
- 5 Lewis Ginter Botanical Garden
- 6 Carytown
- 7 Chesterfield Towne Center
- 8 Cloverleaf Mall
- 9 Greyhound Station
- 10 Hanover Courthouse
- 11 Henrico Courthouse Complex
- 12 Henricus Park
- 13 Historic Chesterfield County Museum
- 14 Magnolia Grange
- 15 McGuire Veterans Hospital
- 16 Meadow Farm Museum/Crump Park
- 17 Paramount's Kings Dominion
- 18 Virginia E. Randolph Museum
- 19 Regency Square
- 20 Richmond Braves, The Diamond
- 21 Richmond International Raceway
- 22 Lora Robins Gallery
- 23 Scotchtown
- 24 The Showplace
- 25 Southside Speedway
- 26 State Fairgrounds on Strawberry Hill
- 27 Swift Creek Mill Playhouse
- 28 Three Lakes Nature Center & Aquarium
- 29 Tuckahoe Plantation
- 30 Virginia Aviation Museum
- 31 Virginia Center Commons
- 32 Virginia House
- 33 Westhampton/The Shops at Libbie & Grove
- 34 Willow Lawn, The Shops at
- 35 Wilton House Museum

X Attractions
X Shopping
X Battlefields
+ Exit #s

Published by

Rockbridge Publishing Company
P.O. Box 351
Berryville, Va 22611
(540) 955-3980

on behalf of

Sabot School, Inc.
6818 W. Grace St.
Richmond, Va 23226
(804) 288-4122

© 1997 Sabot School, Inc.

All rights reserved. No part of this book may be reproduced in any way or by any means without persmission in writing from The Sabot School, with the exception of short passages for review purposes.

Maps courtesy of Metro Richmond Convention and Visitors Bureau

Library of Congress Cataloging-in-Publication Data

Richmond is for children / edited by the parents of the Sabot School.
— 4th ed.
      p.   cm.
  "First edition"—T.p. verso.
  Includes index.
  ISBN 1-883522-19-6
  1. Richmond (Va.)—Guidebooks. 2. Family recreation—Virginia—Richmond—Guidebooks. I. Sabot School (Richmond, Va.)
F234.R53R53 1997
917.55'4510441—dc21   97-18026
                                                                        CIP

10 9 8 7 6 5 4 3 2 1

DEDICATION

To the children of Richmond

and

to Dr. Irene Carney, Director of the Sabot School,
whose clear vision guides our school steadily into the future
and who has touched the lives of our children with magic.

About Sabot School

Since 1972, Sabot School has exemplified innovation in preschool education. Influenced by the British Infant School and Reggio Emilia models of early education, Sabot offers a curriculum based on themes, questions and interests reflected in our students' activities and play. Our program aims to help children to exercise their powers of observing, theorizing, analyzing and refining ideas. Sabot students also learn how to represent their ideas, knowledge and questions through a variety of media. Our goal is to foster learners who are secure, independent, responsible and enthusiastic about learning.

Although Sabot's program is implemented by a faculty of professional educators, Sabot is a parent-governed school. Sabot's students, teachers and parents are all learners and teachers in our school community.

For more information about Sabot School, call Sabot's Director, Dr. Irene Carney, at 288-4122.

Acknowledgments

Heartfelt thanks go to the many people who helped to produce this book. Mark Guncheon was Sabot's Public Relations Director from 1994-1996. Mark worked tirelessly for the duration of his tenure to bring *Richmond is For Children* into the 1990s. Mark designed the 4th Edition, contacted resources, recruited artwork, explored numerous avenues for publishing and marketing this work (finding Rockbridge Publishing as a result), and generally sustained the Board's enthusiasm and support for the project. Mark volunteered this effort during a busy period in his family's life—the completion of his work very nearly coincided with the arrival of his fourth child. Mark's diligent work and creative contributions, and the unending support of his wife, Blair, were crucial to the publication of this 4th Edition.

In June of 1996, Cindy Spangler took over as Public Relations Director. Since then, Cindy has edited portions of the book as well as coordinated the efforts of the numerous volunteers who edited all of the chapters. Cindy has worked with Kathie Tennery of Rockbridge Publishing to establish a mutually beneficial relationship and has devoted careful attention to finalizing all of the many details preliminary to publication. Cindy completed her work just in time for the arrival of her third child. We owe our deepest thanks to both of these dedicated parent volunteers and their (growing!) families.

Thanks, too, to all of our Sabot volunteers for your many, many hours of calling, researching, editing, discussing, planning and dreaming. We could not have created this book without the fine work of these Sabot parents: Maureen Blackwood, Richard Fine, Sandy Henderson, Beth Ann Lucas, David Raine, Terry Rivers, Bill Shobe, Chuck Shimer, Tom Spangler, and Emily Zwicky. Special thanks to Chuck Shimer and Amy Ashworth of Christian and Barton, L.L.P. for their invaluable advice and to Terry Rivers for applying her artistic skills to the creation of the book's cover. Thanks, too, to the Sabot Board, who relentlessly pursued the successful publication of this edition.

The following individuals have helped us to discover Richmond's many offerings for children:

Katherine Tennery, Rockbridge Publishing
Glenn Rose at James River Basin Canoe Livery, Ltd.
Kay Montgomery Taylor at Sherwood Forest Plantation
Dr. Glenn Winters, VCU Community School of the Performing Arts
Katherine Long, Goochland County Historical Society
Reginald A. Cain, Salvation Army
Patrice Ferrell, U.S. Department of the Interior
Mindy L. Huges, Virginia Marine Science Museum
Alice D. Young, curator of Education at Agecroft Hall
Janet Brittain, Petersburg National Battlefield
Richard W. Hogan, Old Dominion Chapter of the National Railway Historical Society
Mary Mitchell Calos, Tourism Director for the City of Hopewell
Patrick Saylor, Colonial Williamsburg Foundation
Don Dale, Virginia Museum of Fine Arts
Sara Lowe at Nauticus, the National Maritime Center
Melissa J. Haines, John Marshall House
Janene Charbeneau, Museum of the Confederacy
Treena Sammons, The Richmond Braves
Margaret J. Tinsley, The Valentine Museum
Nadja Gutowdke, Virginia Historical Society
Lisa B. DaFoe, County of Henrico
James R. Furqueron, The Poe Museum
Denise Pannell, Richmond Children's Museum
Kate Peeples, the Maymont Foundation
Chuck Shimer and Amy Ashworth, Christian and Barton, L.L.P.

Table of Contents

Chapter 1: General Information

General Information 2
Publications 3
Maps 5
Calendars 5
Television 6
Information Centers 6
Recorded Telephone Messages 7

Chapter 2: Our Past

Museums 10
Historic Sites 18
Churches 20
Cemeteries 21
Historic Homes 22
Monument Avenue 26
Other Monuments 29

Chapter 3: Parks and Preserves

City of Richmond 34
Hanover County 48
Henrico County 49
Chesterfield County 52
State Parks and Preserves in Central Virginia 56

Wildlife Preserves and Other Natural Areas 60

Chapter 4: Science and Nature

Science Centers 64
Places of Interest 66
Pick-Your-Own Farms 67
Christmas Trees 71

Chapter 5: Sports

Spectator 76
Participatory 79
    Bicycling 79
    Bowling 81
    Boating, Tubing 82
    Canoeing 83
    Camping 84
    Fishing 84
    Golf Courses 86
    Gymnastics 87
    Hiking 88
    Horseback Riding 91
    Ice-Skating & Sledding 93
    Marathons 94
    Roller-Skating 94
    Skiing 96
    Swimming 96
    Team Sports 99
    Tennis 102

Chapter 6: Performing Arts and Festivities

Theater 104

Film 107
Music 108
Dance 109
Arts Instruction 110
Outdoor Performances and Free Concerts 116
Seasonal Events 117

Chapter 7: Neighbors

Petersburg 128
Central Virginia 128
Historic Triangle 129
Tidewater 133
Mountains 138
Northern Neck 140
Washington, D.C. 140
Amusement Parks 141

Chapter 8: Working World

Airports 144
Arts and Crafts 145
Banking 146
Farms and Greenhouses 146
Food Markets 148
Media 148
Police, Fire Departments, Secret Service 150
Utilities 152
Weather Forecasting and Reporting 153

Chapter 9: Shopping

Museum Shops 156
Books 156

Educational and Art Supplies 158
Toys 160
Hobbies 162
Used Clothing 163
New Clothing 164

Chapter 10: Kids and the Internet

Local and State Interest 168
Colleges and Universities 169
Public Radio and TV 169
Newspapers and Magazines 170
Museums 170
Education Resources for Kids and Parents 171

Appendix:

Recreation Centers and Organizations 174
Libraries 180
Recreational Opportunities for the Handicapped 182
Summer Camps 184
Parenting Centers 188

Index:

Index 191

Chapter 1

General Information
Publications
Maps
Calendars
Television
Information Centers
Recorded Telephone Messages

Hannah Lickey, Age 5
"Once there was a little elephant"

General Information

In this the 4th edition of **Richmond Is for Children**, we endeavor to prove once again that the Richmond metropolitan area is abundant in activities and events for children of all ages. Though usually noted for its significance in the history of the United States, Richmond and the surrounding area serves more than a single purpose with its many battlefields and monuments. It's alive with creativity, excitement and unique resources that make the state capital and its neighboring counties a fantastic environment for raising children.

Like past editions, the contents of this reference book range from some very typical things to do that you'll probably find in any medium size or larger metropolis. But in this edition, we've updated the phone numbers, addresses and names since the last release, added some new, unique listings that may surprise some veteran parents, showcasing the magic that we feel Richmond offers our children.

We've set up the chapters according to themes, included phone numbers with just about every listing that should help you in a pinch when you need an idea for your child or children. There are several caveats before we begin our in-depth exploration of all that Richmond has to offer. Please be aware that with the passage of time, things do change, and that may include various listings within these pages. Also, we have tried to make our research as complete as possible while maintaining certain criteria and a desire for conciseness and accuracy. Therefore, some omissions have occurred. We apologize if your organization was inadvertently left out and would welcome your input on the next edition of the book. Lastly, **whenever we list a phone number without an area code, the area code assumed is 804.**

Special events, one-time activities and other day-to-day goings-on are difficult to keep track of unless you can get some help. The following media information can serve as your guide to more specific information about what you'll find in the remaining chapters.

General Information

Publications

Richmond Parents Monthly Magazine is published for children and parents and distributed free in the Richmond metropolitan area. Issues are theme-oriented and devoted to various topics and seasonal activities, with a timely and lengthy calendar of things to do, coupons, ads and helpful hints for parents. Office at 1910 Byrd Avenue, Suite 106, Richmond (673-5203, Fax 673-5308).

Richmond Times-Dispatch Thursday "Richmond Weekend," calendar & top picks of the coming week's events; Friday entertainment calendar; Saturday "Green Section," calendar & reviews of TV, entertainment, events.

"Discover Richmond" is an annual supplement to the Times-Dispatch distributed in August, covering almost every aspect of metropolitan Richmond life, many entries pertaining to children. Pick up a copy for sale at the newspaper office, 333 East Grace Street 649-6000.

Style Weekly, published and distributed for free on Tuesdays, offers broad coverage of entertainment, events, current museums and gallery exhibits, and arts. Free at groceries, drug stores and advertiser outlets. Call 358-0825 for nearest location.

Style also produces annual supplements that help keep parents up-to-date on the latest seasonal events and special activities. It's a great resource for parents on children's programs and activities around town. Additional copies for sale at Style office, 1118 West Main Street 358-0825 FAX 355-9089.

Richmond Magazine is a slick-covered, monthly publication featuring themed issues, local news and gossip, regular columnists, top-notch writing & a lengthy calendar of things to do in the metro area. 2500 E. Parham Road, Suite 200, Richmond 23228, 261-0034 FAX 261-1047.

Innsbrook Today, published monthly, written about and distributed free in the Innsbrook area. Office at 4701 Cox Road in Glen Allen 346-2782.

Richmond Is for Children

A host of neighborhood and specialty newspapers provide local event information and are important reference sources for details on events and activities:

The Far West End Press 4401 Waterfront Drive, Glen Allen 527-8384

The Goochland Gazette 3052 River Road West, Goochland 556-3135

Hanover Herald-Progress 11293 Air Park Road, Ashland 798-9031

The Jewish News 212 Gaskins Road 740-2000

Mechanicsville Local 7235 Stonewall Parkway 746-1235

Northside Magazine 2900 Hungry Road, Suite 103, Richmond, 23228, 756-7509

Powhatan Today 3833 Old Buckingham Road, Powhatan 23139, 598-4305

Richmond Free Press 101 West Broad Street 644-0496

The West End Connection 4401 Waterfront Drive, Glen Allen 527-8384

Metropolitan Richmond Visitor's Guide is an annual publication of attractions, accommodations, dining and other information for tourists published by the Richmond Convention & Visitors Bureau, 782-2777.

The Guide to Historic Virginia contains maps and information about the area's history and related events. Published monthly April through December. Available at bookstores.

The Guide to Virginia's Civil War contains directories, maps, events and information on Civil War sites throughout the state. Distributed for free at Civil War sites and battlefield parks.

The Insider's Guide to Greater Richmond is a Richmond Times - Dispatch book that is chock full of day trips, neighborhood information and more. Available at bookstores and for sale at the paper.

General Information

Parks, Preserves and Rivers: A Guidebook to Outdoor Adventures in the Capital Region, by Louise L. Burke and Keith F. Ready. 1985. Natural history and recreational facilities available at all area parks and preserves. There are interesting notes on plants, wildlife, history and geology and detailed trail maps for each entry. At libraries and book stores.

Virginia Family Adventure Guide: Great Things to See and Do for the Entire Family, by Candyce H. Stapen. A great reference book for places all over Virginia with phone numbers, hours of operation and places to stay and eat.

Virginia Outdoor Activity Guide, by W. Lynn Seldon. Outdoors fanatics will find just about everything here, including numbers for resources throughout the state.

Virginia Travel Guide A free annual magazine highlighting state attractions. Lists all parks, wildlife management areas, public fishing lakes, state forests. State-wide calendar of events. Available at Visitor Centers, or call 786-4484.

Maps

Well worth its nominal cost, the **Richmond, Virginia and Vicinity Street Map**, published by ADC of Alexandria Inc., will save much time and headache. Available at most convenience stores, or call 703-750-0510.

Also available is "Fast Map," a quite compact foldout map of the city and the state, published for many cities around the country and for sale in bookstores.

Calendars

Metro Richmond Convention & Visitors Bureau produces quarterly compilations of festivals, shows, parades, plays, events and more. Pick one up at one of the three Visitor Centers listed below or call (800) 365-7272.

Downtown Presents A monthly list of activities downtown including the summer's "Big Gig." Available at Visitor Centers and around town, or call 643-2826.

Parks and Recreation Departments offer quarterly schedules of sports programs and classes for children and adults. Classes, which fill up quite fast, usually are not limited to children living within each county; thus it pays to get your hands on a copy of all schedules as soon as they are available. Free at library branches, or call your Parks and Recreation office:

> City of Richmond: 780-6091
> Chesterfield County: 748-1623
> Henrico County: 672-5100
> Hanover County: 798-8062

The Children's Museum of Richmond offers a monthly newsletter for members that includes a colorful calendar of events for each month. 788-4949.

Television

Throughout the day WWBT, Channel 12, runs public service announcements regarding various events in the area, and many of these are related to children and family activities.

Information Centers

Metro-Richmond Visitor Center and Travelland Exit 14 off I-95/64, or one block north of The Diamond on Robin Hood Road, off Boulevard. 358-5511

General Information

Travel counselors and a six-minute video introduce you to Richmond's historic and cultural points of interest, as well as parks, shopping, restaurants, hotels and businesses. While parents are choosing from a multitude of brochures inside, children can climb aboard the old Chesapeake and Ohio Railroad locomotive, caboose and dining car, and an antique fire engine in Travelland Park adjacent to the Visitor Center. Also displayed outside are a rocket ship, fighter plane and steam tractor.

The Bell Tower-Capitol Square, corner of 9th and Bank Street. Hundreds of brochures describing statewide attractions plus helpful counselors. Open Monday-Saturday, 9 a.m.-5 p.m., 648-3146

Visitor Center at the Richmond International Airport 236-3260

Statewide Visitor Centers - Complete list of centers around the state can be found in the *Virginia Travel Guide*, a publication available at the centers listed above.

Ticketmaster The local ticket broker produces calendars featuring current listings of concerts, sporting events and other activities for which they sell tickets. You can pick up a free calendar at any Ticketmaster location or call 262-8100.

Recorded Telephone Messages

Classic Amphitheatre at Strawberry Hill 600 East Laburnum 228-3213

Children's Museum of Richmond 643-KIDO. Hours, fees.

Innsbrook After Hours concert and event hotline: 965-7922

The Richmond Coliseum Coming Events Hotline: 780-4956

XL102/Q94 Info Line Time, date, and entertainment: 756-INFO

The **Adventure Fun Line** Richmond Area Bicycling Assn.: 266-BIKE

National Weather Service River readings & misc.: 757-899-4200

Richmond Ski Club Fun Line 741-FUNN

Science Museum of Virginia 24-hour information: 367-0000

Skywatch Information (weather) 367-8277

Time of Day 844-3711

Time and Temperature 883-6921

WWBT Call 12 line 345-1212, Weather, school closings in inclement weather, mutual communication of newsworthy stories, etc.

Chapter 2

Our Past

> **Museums**
> **Historic Sites**
> **Churches**
> **Cemeteries**
> **Historic Homes**
> **Monument Avenue**
> **Other Monuments**

Malik Banks, Age 5
"Dinosaurs"

Museums

Museums are coming alive for kids by sponsoring the participatory activities they love—getting them involved in creating their own art, presenting dramatizations of history that help children visualize the past, and providing hands-on experiences that spark their curiosity. Unlike the stereotyped visions of boring warehouses filled with dusty remembrances of the past, Richmond's collection of some 40 museums are treasure houses just waiting to be explored. For example, the Virginia Museum of Fine Arts features a children's resource room to provide many new ways for kids to learn about the arts. The Valentine Museum, Meadow Farm, Chesterfield County Museum, the White House of the Confederacy and many of our historic homes have special "living history" days, when docents dressed in period costume demonstrate old-fashioned crafts, games and lifestyles.

Children's Museum of Richmond 740 Navy Hill Drive 788-4949. This home-away-from-home for many parents, toddlers and older children is an invaluable resource. CMR currently offers innovative exhibits and workshops in the arts, humanities, science, education, human services and business. In the permanent exhibit, Playworks enables children to explore the worlds of shopkeepers, bankers, police officers, firefighters, newscasters and surgeons. The children's bank has real vault doors and real "cash" for making deposits. The supermarket houses shelves of "food" for loading into carts and check-out lanes for little shoppers. The health area features an ambulance loading dock and an operating suite. The television studio, WCMR, has moveable camera equipment and a control booth. In StagePlay, boys and girls can fulfill their fantasies with costumes from the dress-up trunk and then take to the stage to improvise. In Art Studio, children can paint on paper, make a collage or create their own masterpieces.

The Cave, CMR's most popular attraction, is one of only about half a dozen fabricated caves in the country. It contains over 400 stalactites, soda straws (delicate stone icicles) and stalagmites. The low temperature setting simulates the coolness of a real Virginia limestone cave. Children wear hard hats with headlamps to explore the dark passages and the narrow crawl space leading to the "subterranean" dome. There are also peephole galleries for viewing fragile structures.

Our Past

The Children's Museum of Richmond has a number of curriculum-based workshops and daily features for eager visitors. Art programs expose children to different visual, literary and performing arts with an emphasis on participating in the artistic process. The Museum is also home to the Dr. Bernard H. and Margery C. Raymond Collection of over 100 antique toys and pieces of children's furniture. To receive a calendar of events, simply contact the museum.

Teens and college students are invited to gain valuable employment experiences working as volunteers. CMR also sponsors many events for families including the acclaimed Peanut Butter 'N Jam concert series and the ever popular All-American Soapbox Derby race.

Open weekdays and weekends. Call for hours. Small fee, under 2 free. Family memberships include unlimited free admission, monthly calendar and 10 percent discounts at the museum store and on workshops and classes. Call to receive a membership brochure. Group rates are available.

[Note: The Children's Museum of Richmond is scheduled to move to a new site adjacent to the Science Museum on Broad Street in 1999.]

American Historical Foundation Museum 1142 West Grace 353-1812. Housed here are the U.S. Marine Raider Museum and the Military Knife and Bayonet Museum which display weapons, uniforms and much more from U.S. military history. Open weekdays. Admission: free.

Black History Museum and Cultural Center of Virginia 00 Clay Street 780-9093. About two blocks from the Maggie Walker House in historic Jackson Ward, this center commemorates the lives, struggles and accomplishments of African-Americans in Virginia from 1619 to the present by becoming a repository of artifacts and records. It is located in the middle of the block between Adams and St. James streets in a structure that housed the Black branch of the Richmond Public Library. Small admission, student discount, open Tuesday through Saturday, 11am-4pm. Closed on holidays. Group tours may be arranged.

Chesterfield County Museum 1101 Ironbridge Road in Chesterfield 748-1026. A reproduction of the original 1750 Chesterfield County Courthouse. Several exhibits relate to the life of the Appomattox and

Monacan Indians native to the area, Sir Thomas Dale's English Settlement of 1611, and the 18th-century Huguenot settlers. Civil and Revolutionary War artifacts. A replica of an old-fashioned country store is featured as well. Changing exhibits feature antique toys, trains and wood carvings. Open Monday-Friday, Sunday afternoons. Small admission, student discount.

Congregation Beth Ahabah Museum 1109 West Franklin Street 353-2668. Exhibits dealing with the history of Richmond's Jewish communities (with emphasis on families of Beth Ahabah congregation) from 1750 to present. Small donation requested. Open Sunday through Thursday. Call for hours.

Edgar Allan Poe Museum 1914-16 East Main Street 648-5523. This retreat into early 19th-century Richmond where the talented writer and poet lived and worked is housed in the oldest structure in Richmond, the Old Stone House, built circa 1737. Poe never lived in the house but did live only blocks from the site. In the back is the "Enchanted Garden," featuring flowers and other plants favored by Poe. Memorabilia and an extensive collection of books and manuscripts would probably be of interest to older children who are familiar with Poe's work. A model depicts Richmond during Poe's lifetime. Open daily, admission fee, discount for students. Closed on Christmas Day.

Elegba Folklore Society Cultural Center 101 East Broad Street 644-3900. The Elegba Society performs not-to-be-missed dance in the metropolitan area and has opened this center as a showcase for various historical artifacts and exhibits related to the cultural arts. They offer a variety of classes and children's enrichment programs. Open weekdays. Donations accepted. Guided tours for a small fee.

Virginia Fire & Police Museum 200 West Marshall Street 644-1849. This Virginia and National Historic Landmark established in 1849 utilizes a staff of volunteers who teach groups of children the proper way to use the "911" service and what to do in an actual fire. More than 350,000 children have gone through the smoke-filled "Down and Out House" to call a 911 dispatcher. Another program teaches fire safety, home security, drug awareness and classroom leadership. You'll also find more than 50 pieces of antique fire fighting equipment there.

Inside the 1849 firehouse are old-fashioned fire trucks, horse-drawn steamers, a ladder wagon with buckets in tow, a police motorcycle, various badges and memorabilia. A volunteer staff of certified fire prevention instructors teach fire safety and give a puppet show called "Firehouse Friends." The puppet show is also taken to schools state-wide upon request. This building housed the first jail in the City of Richmond. Open weekdays. Admission free, donations accepted, but children taking part in the training program are charged a small fee.

Goochland County Historical Center Courthouse Green, Route 6 556-3966. This museum exhibits documents and items relating to local history and is housed in an old stone jail built before the Civil War. Open Tuesday-Friday and by appointment.

Maggie L. Walker House 110½ East Leigh Street 771-2017 or 780-1380. The daughter of a former slave, Maggie Walker was the first woman to found and become president of a bank in the United States. St. Luke Penny Savings Bank continues today as Consolidated Bank and Trust, the oldest surviving black-operated bank in the country. Walker was also active in women's rights and a founder of the Richmond Chapter of the NAACP.

The 25-room house has been restored to its 1930's appearance. It was the Walker family home from 1904 to 1934, and is furnished with family pieces. Free. Open Wednesday-Sunday except Thanksgiving, Christmas and New Year's Day. Advance notice for groups of more than ten is required. Limited wheelchair access.

Magnolia Grange Museum 10020 Ironbridge Road in the Chesterfield Courthouse 796-1479. This Federal-period plantation house built in 1822 is a Virginia Historic Landmark and is on the National register of Historic Places. It features elaborate plasterwork ceilings and greenhouse-like interiors and other examples of 19th-century architecture. Small admission fee, open weekdays and Sundays. Closed holidays.

John Marshall House 818 East Marshall Street 648-7998. Built in 1790, this was the home of John Marshall for 45 years while he served as Secretary of State, Ambassador to France, and Chief Justice of the

Supreme Court. Among the family's furnishings are the snuff box Marshall used during the Revolutionary War and his favorite desk and chair. In the cellar is his judicial robe and Mrs. Marshall's wedding gown. A tour is geared towards those taking it, so children will not be disappointed. A 10-minute film looks at the balance of power in the federal government in 1801 when Marshall became chief justice. Contact the museum for various educational programs for students. Small admission fee, discount for seniors and students, under 7 free.

Meadow Farm Museum, Crump Park Mountain Road and Courtney 672-5520. Children are attracted to the upstairs of the 1810 farmhouse, where the children's bedroom and toys are on display as they may have been found back then. Wind down the back staircase to the basement kitchen. On special occasions biscuits bake on the open hearth. Peek inside the doctor's office in an outbuilding where medical tools used by John Mosby Sheppard between 1844 and 1877 are displayed. In the barnyard there are typical animals of the 1860s including a pig, sheep, horse, chickens, cows and geese.

Visit during one of the many annual events at the park for good food, traditional music and period costumes in their "Living History" series. Innovative tools of the 19th century are demonstrated at the Harvest Festival while ghost stories are told around a campfire during the "Hauntings and Spooky Stories" event. Civil War reenactments are in the spring and fall. There are traditional holiday celebrations with the Old-Fashioned Fourth of July and in December with the Annual Yuletide Fest.

Park admission is free, open dawn to dusk. Small farmhouse admission. Open Tuesday-Sunday noon-4pm. Call for group visits, more information or a calendar of events.

Money Museum 701 East Byrd Street at the Federal Reserve 697-8108. This special place features the history of money, the development of banking and the workings of the Federal Reserve system. Exhibits offer over 600 examples of primitive moneys, ancient coins, gold and silver bars, and original items from the Philadelphia mint. Displays show how money and coins are minted. Free. Open Monday-Friday.

Our Past

Museum in Memory of Virginia E. Randolph 2200 Mountain Road in Glen Allen 261-5029. This special museum commemorates the life of this leader in the education of rural blacks. Randolph taught in the Henrico schools for 57 years, beginning in 1892. She was the recipient of national awards for her innovative industrial arts programs and conducted the first Arbor Day Program in the state of Virginia. In 1976, the museum was named a National Historic Landmark.

The museum cottage, located on the campus of the Virginia Randolph Educational centers, houses a bust of Randolph, many of her personal possessions and a number of photographs taken during her career. Free. Open Monday, Wednesday, Friday, Saturday, and Sunday afternoons, and by appointment.

Museum and White House of the Confederacy 1201 East Clay Street 649-1861. The museum houses the nation's largest Confederate collection. Mementos from the Civil War include weapons, uniforms, soldier and sailor memorabilia, J.E.B. Stuart's saddle and revolver, and a reconstruction of General Robert E. Lee's headquarters. Here you'll see the sword Robert E. Lee was wearing when he surrendered at Appomattox. The staff can offer a special tour of the White House geared for children with advance notice. Call for times. Group programs and outreach programs are also available.

The neoclassical Brockenbrough house next door was the home of Confederate president Jefferson Davis during the war and has been restored to its wartime appearance. Open daily. Admission fee includes guided or self-guided tour. Group rates are available for ten or more people. Discounts for seniors and students. Combined tickets are available. Free parking in the Medical College of Virginia parking deck located at the end of Clay next to the museum.

Old Dominion Railway Museum 102 North Hull Street 233-6237. Train fans can examine the history of railroading in Richmond here at the old Hull Street Passenger Station. Admission free. Saturday and Sunday afternoons

Science Museum of Virginia Please see page 64.

Richmond Is for Children

Valentine Museum 1015 East Clay Street 649-0711. Victorian interior and furnishings on display in the Wickham-Valentine House, built in 1812. Children's exhibits feature Victorian dolls, puzzles, games and puppets.

Special programs for children are held in conjunction with changing exhibits and holidays such as a garden party, an 1880's Christmas celebration and an 18th-century costume exhibit. Children experience the dress play, dancing and behavior of the era through activities such as silhouette cutting, dance workshops, hoop rolling, marbles and jumping rope. Programs are varied and change quite frequently. Open Monday-Saturday and Sunday afternoon. Admission fee. Discount for seniors and students, free for children under 7.

Virginia Aviation Museum Richmond International Airport. 236-3622. Collection of numerous vintage aircraft, all in excellent condition, plus exhibits of people, places and events significant to Richmond's aviation history. There is a 1943 Piper J-3 Cub, one of the best-known aircraft in the world due to the many men who learned to fly in it. The 1930's Vultee V-1 transport is one of the most advanced of the single-engine monoplanes. A World War I SPAD and Captain Dick Merrill's 1930's open cockpit mail plane are also on display. Films are shown daily in 50-seat Benn Theater. There is an extensive aviation library open by appointment including aviation books and magazines. Handicapped access, a museum gift shop and ample free parking. Open daily except Thanksgiving and Christmas. Admission fee, discount for seniors and students, under 3 free. Group rates available at 367-6552.

Virginia Museum of Fine Arts 2800 Grove Avenue 367-0844. One of the finest museums in the country, with many famous collections. Children enjoy the Egyptian and African displays, the Duane Hanson sculpture, delicate china flowers, the Russian Faberge eggs and the fountains. They also enjoy the 20th-century decorative arts in the West Wing—the lively and large pop art in the Lewis Collection, and the sporting art and American Indian paintings in the Mellon Collection.

This is one of a handful of area attractions that are open evening hours. Small children are welcome, strollers available. Free drop-in tours Thursday evenings and Tuesday-Sunday in the afternoon.

Family open houses and children's workshops are offered in conjunction with special exhibits or holidays, including films, special tours and art studio activities, for children through high school age. Watch newspapers for announcements. The **Children's Art Resource Center** makes the museum much more accessible and enjoyable for children. The facility offers a series of year-round programs including classes and family open houses. Call 367-8148 for details.

Tours can be arranged to fit your group's interests and ages; for example, Animals in Art, grades K-3, includes participatory activities and explores how animal images are used as symbols to tell stories and to decorate useful objects, from ancient to modern times.

Group visits and guided tours for 10-100 can be arranged from October-May. Schedule at least three weeks in advance. Tours may be arranged for selected galleries of your choice, a special exhibition or highlights from the permanent collection. For the physically disabled, visually impaired or hearing impaired, special group tours can be arranged by calling three weeks in advance 367-0859.

The Museum Reference Library (located in the south wing of the Virginia Museum) is open to the public Tuesday through Saturday. Call 367-0827 for more information.

Gallery hours: Tuesday-Sunday 11am-5pm; Thursday until 8pm. Closed Mondays and New Year's Day, Fourth of July, Thanksgiving Day and Christmas Day. Museum Shop: Tuesday-Saturday 10:30am-4:30pm; Sunday 2pm-4:30pm (mid-June to Labor Day: Tuesday-Saturday 1pm-3:30pm; Sunday 2pm-4:30pm).

Admission free, suggested donation $4.00 (special exhibitions might require an additional fee.)

The Virginia Historical Society 428 North Boulevard 358-4901. Battle Abbey, a 1912 memorial to the Confederate soldier, houses the headquarters for the Virginia Historical Society, the oldest continuously operating institution in the commonwealth of Virginia. Known for its monumental murals, the holdings of the Society form the most comprehensive collection of Virginians in existence. Among artifacts in the six galleries are Confederate flags, uniforms and buttons; and china portraits from the 17th and 18th centuries. There are changing exhibits and programs including their latest, "The Story of Virginia," which features Pocahontas's buttons, George Washington's diary, and Virginia's "Liberty Bell."

The Research Library contains manuscripts and documents concerning state history and is open to the public.

Galleries and library open Monday through Saturday. Galleries only, Saturday afternoons. Handicap accessible. Small admission fee, discount for students.

Virginia Telephone Museum 3520 Ellwood Avenue 772-5921. The Richmond Life Member Club of the Old Dominion Chapter #43 of the Telephone Pioneers maintains this museum and its collection of items relating to the heritage of the telephone. Open the first Friday and the third Wednesday of every month from 10am-3pm. Group tours can also be arranged by calling 741-1449.

Historic Sites

Capitol Square Ninth and Grace Streets. One of the prettiest spots downtown, with fountains and cobblestone paths among shade trees so tall they compete with nearby buildings, like the Washington Building at the bottom of the hill on Bank Street. There is a small snack bar inside the state building, on the first floor, open on weekdays. Children can chase the squirrels and feed the pigeons. Sometimes, in warm weather, there is entertainment on the grounds at lunch time.

Governor's Mansion Capitol Square 371-2642. Virginia's executive mansion is the oldest continuously occupied governor's residence in the United States built for that purpose. Built in 1813. Free and open to the public for 15-minute tours by appointment only. The tour schedule changes by season; please call 371-TOUR for the current times.

There is usually an open house at Christmastime to view traditional decorations, and during April for Garden Week. Groups should call in advance for reservations.

Pioneer Farmstead State Fairgrounds 228-3268. During the State Fair, there is a family in residence to show what life was like 200 years ago in Virginia. They make apple butter, wash clothes and perform other chores as done in pioneer days. There are six buildings on the farmstead:

cabin, springhouse, barn, outhouse, henhouse, and combination workshop and root cellar. The buildings remain all year and are open to visitors.

Richmond National Battlefield Park Chimborazo Visitors Center, 3215 East Broad Street 226-1981. Ten National Park units commemorate the defense of Richmond during the Civil War. Start at the Chimborazo Visitors Center, named after the Chimborazo General Hospital, where there are exhibits, a slide show entitled "Battlefields Around Richmond," and a short introductory film, "Richmond Remembered." There are tour maps here and a schedule of living history programs taking place throughout the year.

Smaller visitors centers are at Cold Harbor and at Fort Harrison. There are audio stations, paintings and interpretive signs at Chickahominy Bluff, Malvern Hill, Fort Harrison and Drewery's Bluff. The Watt House, Gaines' Mill, Fort Harrison, Fort Brady and Drewery's Bluff have short, self-guiding trails to hike past old earthen fortifications and other historical points of interest.

You can also rent or buy an auto tape tour and booklet at Chimborazo for the Seven Days' Campaign and tour the battlefields at your own pace. The 60-mile trip takes about three hours.

There are picnic facilities at Fort Harrison and Cold Harbor. For more information call 226-1981. See also listings for Chimborazo Park and Nature, Environmental Activities Related to History.

Admission free. Open daily.

Virginia State Capitol Ninth and Grace Streets 786-4344. Designed by Thomas Jefferson in 1785 in the style of a Roman temple, the Capitol houses the oldest law-making body in the western hemisphere—the General Assembly of Virginia. There is a 30-minute guided tour of the Old House of Delegates, the Senate and House chambers and the Rotunda, featuring the only statue of George Washington done from life, by Houdon. There are also busts of seven other Virginia-born presidents.

Children should have some background in American and Virginian history. Best for 4th grade and up. Tours given all day until 4:15pm. Schedule group tours 4-6 weeks in advance. Free. Open Monday-Saturday, 9am-5pm; Sunday (during December-March) 1pm-5pm. Closed Christmas Day.

Virginia War Memorial Belvidere Avenue, just north of the Lee Bridge. Virginia's memorial to her World War II and Korean War dead is an open pavilion of marble and glass overlooking the James River. Thousands of names are inscribed on the walls, and a figure of a weeping woman represents Virginia mourning. Ample parking.

From here you can walk to Gambles Hill—down steps to the east, across a bridge and up the hill. To walk to Riverside Park, follow the road under the Lee Bridge.

Churches

Monumental Church 13th and East Broad Street. Built on the site of the Richmond Theater, in memorial to the 72 people who died when the theater burned to the ground on December 26, 1811. Two men—Dr. James McCaw and a slave blacksmith, Gilbert Hunt—are remembered for bravely saving the lives of the 600 people who were attending the play on the evening of the fire. The church, now owned by the Historic Richmond Foundation, is not open for tours except upon special request at 780-0107.

Students of black history will be interested in knowing that a detailed account has been written about Gilbert Hunt's life, which encompassed many facets of antebellum black life in Richmond. Hunt developed his skills as a blacksmith and was eventually able to buy his freedom and establish a smithing business. He acquired a considerable amount of property, including slaves of his own. He was a leader in the black church at a time when it played many roles in enhancing the lives of its members and the community. You can read about Gilbert Hunt in the Valentine Museum's exhibition catalog "In Bondage and Freedom, Black Life in Richmond, Va."

Old Blanford Church 733-2396. The oldest building in Petersburg with a clearly documented history, dating from at least 1735. It features 15 world-famous Tiffany stained glass windows, each donated by a different Southern state to commemorate native sons who died in the Civil War. The first Memorial Day was observed here in June 1866. Tours available for a small fee. Guided tours of historic Blanford Cemetery available.

St. John's Episcopal Church 2401 East Broad Street 648-5015. This is where Patrick Henry made his "Give me liberty or give me death" speech during the Second Virginia Convention, March 23, 1775, before the outbreak of the Revolutionary War. Each year on the Sunday closest to the anniversary, a commemorative reenactment is held, in costume. Other reenactments are held every Sunday from Memorial Day through Labor Day at 2pm. Arrive early for balcony seating. 18th-century frame church and furnishings.

On the cemetery grounds surrounding the church are the graves of George Wythe, a signer of the Declaration of Independence, and Elizabeth Arnold Poe, Edgar Allan Poe's mother.

Small admission fee, discount for seniors and students, under 7 free. Open Monday-Saturday 10am-3:30pm, Sundays 1pm-4pm.

St. Paul's Episcopal Church 815 East Grace Street. Robert E. Lee and Jefferson Davis worshipped here during the Civil War. Open 10am-4pm, Monday-Saturday. Chapel services Monday-Friday at noon. Located across the street from the entrance to Capitol Square.

St. Peter's Church 800 East Grace Street. Oldest Roman Catholic Church in the city (1834). Daily Mass. Monday-Saturday 9am-4pm; Sunday 7am-3pm.

Cemeteries

Franklin Street Burying Grounds 2000 East Franklin Street. Thought to be the oldest Jewish cemetery in the country; dates back to 1791.

Hebrew Cemetery Fourth and Hospital Streets. Rows of stacked rifles and crossed sabers fence the Confederate section of this cemetery, established in the early 1800's and still in use. Located across from Shockoe Hill Cemetery.

Hollywood Cemetery 412 South Cherry Street 648-8501. With its beautiful landscaping, old trees and interesting monument epitaphs, this riverside cemetery is a pleasant place to stroll. Many famous people in Virginia and United States history are buried here, including two presidents, James Monroe and John Tyler. Also interred here are Confederate president Jefferson Davis, General J.E.B. Stuart and Commodore Matthew Fontaine Maury. The graves of 18,000 Confederate soldiers are commemorated by one huge pyramidal monument made of stacked stones. For a map of the historic section, stop at the headquarters inside the entrance. Gates are open daily 8am- 5pm, Office is open Monday through Friday 8:30am-4:30pm. Pick up a brochure including a tour map here.

Oakwood Cemetery 3101 Nine Mile Road 780-4473. Burial grounds of 17,000 Confederate soldiers. Open 7 am to dusk.

Shockoe Hill Cemetery 201 Hospital Street 780-4465. Buried here are Chief Justice John Marshall; Elmira Shelton, the inspiration of Poe's "Lost Lenore"; and Revolutionary War hero Peter Francisco. Open 7am-dark.

Historic Homes

(Some historic homes are listed elsewhere in this guide—such as Chapter 4, Science and Nature, and Chapter 3, Parks and Preserves—if services other than their historic value is their primary attraction.)

Some of America's oldest and grandest homes are right here in Richmond. Their unique design, original and reproduction furnishings, family portraits and memorabilia reflect the lifestyles of bygone days. Those days come alive for children when they can see and hear about the things that were used by former occupants in their daily lives—their tools, cooking utensils, school books and toys. Ages 10 and older best appreciate touring inside. Younger children have fun exploring interesting outbuildings—barns and sheds, school rooms, detached kitchens—or roaming through boxwood mazes and herb gardens.

Plan a December visit, when Yuletide greenery, seasonal music, traditional foods and candlelight tours add drama to the occasion. Come during Garden Week in April to see gardens in their finest bloom. Watch newspapers for announcements.

Besides the homes described here, you may want to visit:

Scotchtown, Patrick Henry's home during the Revolutionary War; ten miles west of Ashland, Route 685.

Edgewood and Sherwood Forest Plantations, both on Route 5.

Westover, adjacent to Berkeley and open only during Garden Week.

Obtain brochures with more information about the Visitor Centers at Capitol Square (see Information Centers, Bell Tower).

Agecroft Hall 4305 Sulgrave Road 353-4241. Agecroft Hall was originally constructed outside of Manchester, England, as a manor house in the early 16th century. Mr. and Mrs. Thomas C. Williams, Jr., of Richmond, Virginia, purchased the house at auction in 1925. The best building materials from the manor were shipped to Virginia, where the Williams' architect incorporated them into a modern house constructed between 1926 and 1928. Opened as an historic house museum in 1969, Agecroft Hall is situated on a 23-acre site overlooking the James River. The museum collection includes objects made and/or used in England during the 16th and 17th centuries. The museum also offers a thematic tour on food and dining customs of the period called "Bellycheer: Dining in England 1580-1640" twice a day.

A visit includes a 10-minute slide orientation and a 30-45-minute guided tour. Visitors are encouraged to take a self-guided tour of the gardens and grounds including the formal sunken garden, as well as the recreated 17th-century knot, herb, fragrance and Tradescant gardens.

The education department offers special school programs for elementary and secondary students as well as a wide range of public programs for adults and families. Occasionally the museum offers living history events with costumed interpreters portraying the residents of family in a special tour called "Tudor Tykes."

Open year-round, Tuesday through Saturday and Sunday afternoons. Admission fee, discount for seniors and students, children under 6 free. Garden only tickets are available for half price. Discounts are available for pre-booked groups of ten or more. Please call for more information.

Berkeley Plantation 12602 Harrison Landing Road in Charles City 829-6018. In 1619, English settlers stepped ashore at Berkeley and held the first Thanksgiving Day feast more than a year before Pilgrims arrived in New England. An exciting time for families to visit Berkeley is the first Sunday in November, when Virginia's First Thanksgiving is celebrated. Festivities for the annual event include reenactments, music, food, activities and special tours.

The oldest three-story brick house in Virginia, Berkeley was built in 1726 by Benjamin Harrison. His son, Col. Benjamin, was a signer of the Declaration of Independence and three-time governor of Virginia. Further generations produced two presidents, William Henry Harrison (Old Tippecanoe) and his grandson, Benjamin, all of whom lived in the ancestral home and entertained many famous people of their day. "Taps" was composed here in 1862.

The site offers a Civil War museum, terraced gardens, slide presentation and guided tours. During summer months a tavern is open for lunch.

Open daily except Christmas. Admission fee, discount for seniors and students, under 6 free. Additional fee for Thanksgiving festivities. Located 25 miles east of Richmond on Route 5, just east of Ben Harrison Bridge (Route 156).

Centre Hill Mansion Adams and Tabb Streets in Petersburg 733-2401. An 1823 Federal mansion depicting the elegance of antebellum Southern living, Centre Hill has been host to three United States presidents. Of particular interest is the 1886 grand piano in the front parlor and the reenactment of the 1864 "Starvation Ball." An annual ghost watch occurs on January 24th. Will the Civil War brigade appear or not?

Shirley Plantation 501 Shirley Plantation Road in Charles City 829-5121, (800) 232-1613. Settled six years after Jamestown was established, this 800-acre working plantation is operated by the tenth generation of the original owners. During the Revolutionary War, the plantation was a supply center and listening post between the British at City Point and Lafayette's army at Malvern Hill. Robert E. Lee's mother was born at Shirley nearly a century later, and the famous general attended classes in the converted laundry room. The National Historic Landmark is still a working plantation today.

Among the many architectural treasures and furnishings inside the house is a carved walnut staircase, rising three stories without visible means of support. It is the only one of its kind in America.

The Shirley grounds afford an expansive view of the river and make a relaxing picnic spot. You can see many of the interesting outbuildings free, including barns, smokehouse, dovecote and an unusual ice cellar.

Open daily except Christmas and Thanksgiving Day; last tour begins at 4:30pm. Admission fee, discount for students, children under 6 free.

Tuckahoe Plantation 12601 River Road 784-5736. One of the finest and most complete 18th-century plantations, Tuckahoe, boyhood home of Thomas Jefferson, has been a home and working farm for nearly 275 years. Among the rare outbuildings in this National Historic Landmark are the office and schoolhouse where Jefferson attended classes. The home is beautifully furnished and contains many architectural embellishments. With its several outbuildings, Tuckahoe is one of the most complete colonial plantation layouts in North America.

The annual Christmas celebration, held the second Saturday in December, hosts hayrides and a bonfire, candlelight tour by costumed docents, handbell chorus, roaring fires and hot apple cider and holiday decor.

Open by appointment only, any day except holidays. The tour and walk around the grounds takes about an hour and a half. School groups may picnic on the lawn. Located 4.6 miles west of Parham Road on River Road.

Virginia House 4301 Sulgrave Road 353-4251. Reconstructed in 1925 from brick shipped from England, the house exhibits characteristics of both the 1125 English monastery and the 1547 English house from which its building materials were taken. Elizabethan and Tudor art, furnishings and artifacts are on display inside. Children enjoy seeing the suit of armor and the weaponry from the 15th-18th centuries and the goldfish pond in the garden. The wild garden featuring wildflowers and meadows along the James River and the "pleasances" are fun to explore and admire.

Open daily Tuesday through Saturdays and Sunday afternoons. Admission fee, discount for students and children. Group tours, by appointment only, concern the history of the family who built the house and how they acquired the furnishings.

Wilton House Museum 215 South Wilton Road 282-5936. This stately Georgian mansion was built between 1750 and 1753 and was used by General Lafayette as his headquarters during part of the Revolutionary War. The house was moved to its present location in 1935 from a location east of Richmond on the James River. Among many original furnishings are 17th- and 18th-century replacement pieces and family portraits. The parlor is considered to be one of the most beautiful rooms in America. In the nursery is an antique doll set. Tours for groups of children are presented by special docents who interpret 18th-century family life. Guides will also tailor tours to your interests. Annual candlelight tour in December.

Admission fee, discount for seniors and youths, children under 6 free. Open Tuesday-Saturday and Sunday afternoons with the last tour at 3:45pm.

Dooley Mansion, see Maymont

Monument Avenue

One of the most beautiful of Southern boulevards, Monument Avenue is named for the six monuments commemorating heroes that grace the street's park-like median. Take a family walk down the 1.3 miles from the Maury monument at Belmont Avenue to the Stuart statue at Lombardy

Street. End your hike a block south at the corner of Lombardy and Park Avenue with a romp in the tot-lot across the street.

As you walk along, play a game of identifying the columns on the houses. The three most common architectural types are Doric, Ionic and Corinthian. You may also want to bring a pair of binoculars to examine the details on monuments you can't get close to, like the Maury.

Another fun way to enjoy the avenue is to join the Easter Parade, held annually on Easter Sunday (see Seasonal Events).

Arthur Ashe Monument Monument Avenue and Roseneath Street. The Arthur Ashe Monument is the first addition to Monument Avenue since 1929. It was officially erected on July 10, 1996. It was sculpted in bronze by local artist Paul Di Pasquale honoring Richmond's own Arthur Ashe. Ashe, athlete, author and humanitarian, is depicted holding books and a tennis racquet, teaching the children who sit around him.

The Ashe monument is the only statue on the Avenue that is not of a Confederate general. Arthur Ashe is the first African-American to be honored on this avenue.

Matthew Fontaine Maury Monument Monument Avenue and Belmont Avenue. Confederate Navy Commodore Maury charted air and sea currents and is attributed with founding the sciences of meteorology and geography. Children may recognize this monument as "the melted ice cream cone" approaching from the west, and it is fairly dripping with allegory. Older kids may enjoy spotting the many symbols.

The monument, according to sculptor F. W. Sievers, is a tribute to Maury's desire to improve the lot of the mariner and the farmer. Maury is seated, "listening to the terrors of a storm," and foresees the usefulness of charting sea and air currents. Behind him are scenes of a shipwreck and a farm family fleeing the storm—looking for help from Maury. Sea lanes and calms identified by Maury are etched on the surface of the bronze globe. Dolphins symbolize "the coming of relief." Saltwater fish on the plinth stand for Maury's investigation of the sea; the shells, the mapping of the ocean floor and the fresh water fish on the base, his study of inland waterways.

Swallows and bats swirling on the pedestal symbolize the atmosphere, as well as successive day and night. On two lower corners are carved electric rays, or torpedo fish. Maury invented the electric torpedo. His inspiration for this invention supposedly came while playing with a bar of soap in his bathtub at his house on Clay Street.

Thomas J. "Stonewall" Jackson Monument Monument Avenue and Boulevard. Broadly acclaimed as the Confederacy's greatest general next to Lee, General Jackson and his brigade won renown (and a nickname) by standing "like a stone wall" at the first battle of Bull Run.

The general died at Guinea Station south of Fredericksburg after being wounded in the Chancellorsville battle, contrary to the inscription. Jackson and his horse, Little Sorell, are immortalized facing the North, in keeping with the traditional orientation of statues of Southern heroes killed in the Civil War.

The head of the statue was modeled from the death mask taken by sculptor Frederick Volk. You can see the mask at the Valentine Museum. The monument itself is the work of F. William Sievers, who also designed the Maury monument ten years later in 1929.

Jefferson Davis Monument Monument Avenue and Davis Avenue. Davis was, of course, the first and only president of the Confederate States of America. Here, the great orator and exponent of constitutional rights stands with the right hand raised as if making a point in a speech. His left hand rests on a copy of the Constitution of the United States, which sits atop the traditional column of the Confederacy.

Behind the Davis figure is a semicircle of 13 Doric columns representing the 13 Confederate states. Towering over this cluster is the mythological female figure, "Vindicatrix, the Protector," on a 67-foot pedestal. A woman's figure is often used in art to symbolize an ideal or a virtue—in this case, justice. The motto of the Confederacy, inscribed here, was "Deo Vindice," God Our Protector.

The Richmond artist Edward V. Valentine designed and sculpted this monument in his studio, which has been preserved at the Valentine Museum. There is an old story that the young woman who modeled for "Vindicatrix" married the model for Valentine's statue of Lee in the United States Capitol Building, and that the couple met in Valentine's studio.

Robert E. Lee Monument Monument Avenue and Allen Avenue. This bronze figure of the commander of the Army of Virginia on his steed, Traveller, was the first monument to be constructed on the avenue. A year or two prior to its unveiling in May 1890, the area was still mostly grassy meadow. At the time, there was local concern that the monument be at least as high as the George Washington monument on the Capitol grounds (it is exactly one foot taller).

The large pedestal was built to enable the addition of more figures later, possibly Lee's lieutenants, though they never were added.

Sculpted by Jean Antoine Mercie, the statue was built and first viewed in France before being shipped to this country. When the figure arrived by train to Richmond it came in separate castings, and the parts were hauled through the streets by school children and others. Thousands gathered to put their hands to the big ropes used to draw the vehicles containing the parts. Many cut bits of this rope and kept them for souvenirs. A few of these are in the permanent collection at the Museum of the Confederacy.

Since Lee "lived to help heal the South," his statue is oriented toward the South.

J.E.B. Stuart Monument Monument Avenue and Lombardy Street. A dramatic pose of Gen. Stuart on his galloping mount, and an appropriate memorial to the Confederate calvary commander known for his brilliant raids and daring deeds.

There is an old dispute about whether the statue, by Fred Moynihan, is an original work of art or a copy of a similar monument sculpted by Moynihan's mentor, John Henry Foley. That monument, of tiger-hunter Sir James Outram, British general of the Indian Mutiny, is in Calcutta. A few blocks from Stuart Circle, at 210 West Grace Street, is the house where Stuart died of wounds he received near Yellow Tavern while defending Richmond from Sheridan's army.

The statue was unveiled in the spring of 1907 by Stuart's little granddaughter, Virginia Stuart Waller, before a great crowd of cheering Confederate veterans.

Other Monuments

James Center Plaza Cary Street and 9th and 10th Streets. Located precisely where the Turning Basin of the canal system was from 1785 to the 1850's, developer Henry Faison was inspired to create this plaza in the European tradition of a central meeting place with art integrating the history of the site.

> **Wind's Up** This bronze grouping by artist Lloyd Lillie depicts three 8-foot muscular figures pulling the halyards to hoist the sails. The 50-foot mast and sail tower over a stone deck and pond.
>
> **Boatman's Tower** A 25 brass-bell carillon atop a limestone tower. The bronze barge man and mule draw a boat upriver, rotating when the bells chime the hour and half-hour with seasonal melodies. The seating arrangement nearby is made from old Kanawha Canal stones, placed to suggest the shape of a typical lock.

Christmas is an especially good time to visit the plaza with small children, when 78 life-size sculptured deer and trees strung with more than 6,000 strands of lights create an enchanting effect. Decorations go up the first weekend after Thanksgiving.

Model trains and other railroad exhibits are on display inside the James Center, usually the last two weeks before Christmas, until around 8:30pm weekdays and Saturdays, and Sundays 1 p.m.-5 p.m. To verify hours, call 344-3222.

Bojangles West Leigh and Chamberlayne Avenue. Erected in 1973, this statue portrays Bill Robinson, the famous Richmond-born tap dancer, dancing down a flight of stairs.

Liberty Chimborazo Park. Miniature of the Statue of Liberty (8.5 ft.), donated by the Boy Scouts of America in 1951 and recently restored.

Sundial Hampton Street and Pennsylvania Avenue. Eight-sided stepped shaft, 20 feet high, located outside the Hampton Street entrance to Maymont. The south face contains a working, upright sundial with inscribed directions for its use.

Three Bears 12th and Broad Street. A stone grouping of three small bears playing with twigs in the small, walled-in park in front of MCV's West Hospital. The bears symbolize the healing gods of some Native Americans.

Police Memorial Nina Abady Festival Park, 6th Street Marketplace. Bronze, 8-foot-tall statue depicting a city patrolman stepping down a red granite stair. He is holding a child, who is clutching a teddy bear. A plaque in front lists the names of the 26 Richmond officers who have died on duty. The artist is Maria Kirby-Smith of Philadelphia.

Richmond Is for Children

Chapter 3

Parks and Preserves

City of Richmond
Hanover County
Henrico County
Chesterfield County
State Parks and Preserves in Central Virginia
Wildlife Preserves and Other Natural Areas

Elizabeth Poole, Age 6
"Deer at Maymont Park"

City of Richmond

Parks

The city of Richmond features one of the oldest municipal park systems in the country, one that got its start back in 1851 when the Richmond City Council voted to acquire 7.5 acres that are now known as Monroe Park. Libby Hill Park came next. Today, there are more than 40 parks with a total of more than 1,500 acres. On those acres and throughout the city itself, more than a quarter of a million trees grow, giving Richmond the title of Tree City, USA. The departments of Parks, Recreation and Community Facilities offer more than 20 community centers with varied classes and programs, indoor and outdoor swimming pools, and other facilities that gear their programs toward children. For information on other recreation specialties of Parks and Recreation, call:

Martial arts - Tracy Fleming, 780-6006
Swim team - Richard Tyree, 780-6174
Tennis - Mr. Junie Chatman, 780-8116
Soccer - Jimmie Bierne, 780-6175
Football - Milton Marshall, 780-4126
Dance - Annette Holt, 780-6047
Art - Darlene Marschak, 780-6089

West end

Byrd Park Boulevard Avenue, just north of Boulevard Bridge. Three lakes for fishing, feeding ducks and paddleboating, tree-shaded lawns and open fields, tennis courts and ball fields. Dogwood Dell Festival of the Arts, the city's free, outdoor performing arts series takes place here at the amphitheater in the summertime (see Outdoor Concerts, Dogwood Dell). The Carillon, a World War I memorial located nearby, is used as a recreation center and art gallery. Children's performances are held behind the Carillon on summer Sundays at the Ha' Penny Stage. Within sight is a playground for toddlers.

Parks and Preserves

The park's asphalt trails are fine for strolling, biking and jogging. There are several Vita-course exercise stations along the way. Rent paddleboats in the summer for fun rides. Winter brings sledding to the hillsides around Fountain Lake.

There are picnic shelters and grills around the lakes and parking on streets unless designated otherwise. Restrooms are in the field house near the tennis courts and in the Carillon. Most of the park is accessible to wheelchairs.

Petronius S. Jones Park 1400 block of Idlewood Avenue. Features playground, basketball and tennis courts, plus a walking trail.

Maymont 1700 Hampton Street, adjacent to Byrd Park 358-7166. Much more than a traditional park, Maymont is a 100-acre Victorian country estate including the Children's Farm; Native Virginia Wildlife Exhibits; opulent Maymont House museum; Carriage Collection and carriage rides; beautiful Italian, Japanese and Herb Gardens. Large, open hillsides and shady picnic areas. Family-oriented activities celebrate every holiday and season.

The Children's Farm is at the Spottswood Street entrance. This "petting zoo" is populated with cows, pigs, goats, sheep, donkeys, llamas, rabbits, peacocks and colorfully plumed chickens with an emphasis on rare and endangered breeds. Healthful animal food is dispensed from gumball machines, so bring small change for feeding. A few shade trees and a concession stand in the Farm area provide respite from the summer heat. The animals are on display Tuesday-Sunday from 12-5pm.

The Wildlife Exhibits are scattered below the Children's Farm. Here you can see animals native to Virginia in natural habitats—deer and elk on the hillside and gray fox and owls, hawks and other birds of prey along the path to the right after the bridge. Black bear are at the bottom of the path, and beyond is the Japanese Garden. Children will enjoy the stepping-stones and the huge koi—or goldfish—in the pond.

If you have small children with you or a stroller, double back to the bridge. At this point, instead of recrossing, go straight to the Aviary and the Bison Habitat before returning to your car. The more vigorous can continue beyond the Japanese Garden, up a very steep set of stairs alongside the waterfall to the Italian Garden, Maymont House and the Nature Center.

The Mary Parsons Nature Center is one of the most exciting educational centers for children in the Richmond area, and it's a great rainy-day spot as well. Easily reached by the Hampton Street entrance and housed in a stone barn to the left, exhibits illustrate the habitats, life cycles and food chains of animals. The Discovery Room has carpeted floors and platforms that encourage children to sit and leisurely examine and play with hands-on exhibits—puzzles, blocks, puppets, shells and skulls, insects and small animals encased in plastic. Terrariums are at children's eye-level, and many can be walked around for better viewing. Feeding time is a good time to see slow-moving or timid creatures in action (call for schedule). Also in the Nature Center, three types of freshwater wetlands—swamps, marshes and bogs—are represented. The central focus of the exhibit is a round, 650-gallon freshwater aquarium, 8 feet in diameter. The tank is filled with huge carp, catfish, perch, bass, pickerel and other fish and turtles. Fun and educational programs are offered throughout the year for all ages and interests, and day camps are offered in the summer. The Nature Center is open Tuesday-Sunday from 12-5pm, September-May and 10am-5pm, June-August. Donations requested.

Maymont House, built in 1893 in opulent Victorian style, is open for tours year round. Special tours make the House fun for children, including the monthly "Discover Maymont House" tour which features the animal images hidden in the decoration of the Dooley Mansion. During the annual Christmas Open House when the House is at its most beautiful, Victorian traditions are celebrated with yule logs, wassail and ginger cookies, costumed tour guides, carolers, bell ringers and visits from Father Christmas. Sign up at the Hampton Street gate for free House tours and carriage rides. Maymont House is open Tuesday-Sunday from 12-5pm, September-May and 10am-5pm, June-August. Donations requested.

The Maymont Shop, near the mansion, sells Victorian jewelry, toys and garden-related items. Another concession stand, drinking fountains and restrooms are here, too.

Most of the park is easily accessible to the handicapped in wheelchairs. Avoid steep hills below the Children's Farm by going to the left past the bison. Restrooms at the Children's Farm and Maymont Shop provide handicapped access.

Brief carriage rides, and tram tours of the whole estate, are available for a small fee in the warmer months, weather permitting. Call for schedule. (Maymont members ride the tram for free.)

Maymont's grounds and gardens are open every day of the year, 10am-5pm, November through March; and 10am-7pm, April through October. Indoor exhibits including the Nature Center, Maymont House and the Children's Farm Barn are closed Mondays; open Tuesday-Sunday from 12-5pm. The exhibits open at 10am on Tuesday-Saturday in June, July and August. The last Maymont House tour begins at 4:30pm.

Directions: To the Hampton Street Entrance (nearest the Nature Center, Maymont House and Gardens) – South on the Boulevard, left on Cary Street. Take a right on Meadow Street. Go one mile to Pennsylvania Avenue and take a right, then go one block to Hampton Street parking lot. To the Spottswood Entrance (nearest the Children's Farm and Wildlife Exhibits) – South on the Boulevard to the Columbus Statue and take a right. Take a left on Pumphouse Drive at the Carillon, left onto Shirley and right into the Spottswood parking lot.

Maymont is admission free. Operated by the private, nonprofit Maymont Foundation, donations and volunteers are always welcome. Many historical, environmental and gardening classes and workshops are offered for a fee at Maymont throughout the year, including the few listed below. For a schedule of events, call 358-7166.

Become a member of the Maymont Foundation and receive newsletters and discounts on classes.

A Family Easter at Maymont, with pony rides, bonnet contests, egg hunts, face painting and the Easter Bunny, make this a great way to spend Easter Sunday.

Musical Mondays at Maymont is a series of free concerts featuring brass bands held on the Carriage House Lawn on six Monday evenings in July and August. Many listeners bring a picnic.

The Great Big Crazy Camp Out is offered by the Nature Center in June and offers families the chance to pitch a tent and spend the night discovering Maymont's nighttime animals through games, singing and activities. Other indoor camp-ins are offered as well.

Gambles Hill and Riverside Parks Two of Richmond's oldest parks afford sweeping views of the James River and the Kanawha Canal.

Gambles Hill 2nd and Arch Street, is now owned by the Ethyl Corporation, but the public may walk through. This is a good place to get an overview of the Tredegar Iron Works. Drive south to the end of 3rd Street and park on the street. To walk to the Virginia War Memorial from here, go south on 2nd Street, cross the bridge and take the steps up the hill to the monument.

Oregon Hill Park, formerly Riverside Park, is across from the Virginia War Memorial on Belvidere. From here you see another view of the James, the canal and Belle Isle.

Steps near the western edge of the park lead down to the old towpath where mules once pulled boats up the canal. You can walk underneath the Lee Bridge along a one-way street to the War Memorial. Oregon Hill Park is only a few blocks from the Hollywood Cemetery.

Great Shiplock Park Pear Street. The Great Shiplock was the first series of locks called the Tidewater Connection that lifted boats around the rapids and shallows of the Falls of the James. Kiosks in the park tell the story of the building of the canal system. The seven-mile stretch from Richmond to Westham was completed in 1795 and included the Great Basin. This basin was a wide pool that allowed boats to dock, unload and turn around. Located where the CSX James River Center is today, it was the center of the commercial district.

The original plan for the canal, and the dream of George Washington, was to make navigation possible from Richmond to the Ohio River connecting the James River and the Great Kanawha River in West Virginia. The waterway was completed to Buchanan, on the western slopes of the Blue Ridge, by 1851, and reached its peak of activity and prosperity in the late 1850s. During the Civil War the canal underwent much damage, and competition with railroads eventually brought an end to the use of the canal system as an economical way to transport goods. The Richmond and Allegheny Railroad bought the property in 1878, and the canal was filled in or allowed to go dry.

At this small park on the wooded island created by the canal, you can observe the workings of the old lock gates. There are paths along the river bank and through the forest, and frequent trains can be seen approaching a half-mile down the trestle. Take care at the southern end of the lock, because there is no fence around the top of the wall, leaving exposed a 20-foot drop to the rocky riverbed below.

To get to the park, take East Main Street to the 2700 block, then go right on Pear Street to the park at the dead end.

Kanawha Canal Lock Park 12th and Byrd Street. The Canal Walk opens up an interesting and fun area of the city to explore and provides a different perspective from which to view the city and learn about its industrial development and dependence on the river. The Canal Walk winds its way through downtown, marked by flags and plaques. A good place to start with children is Kanawha Park, located where Byrd Street dead-ends at 12th Street at Reynolds Metal Co. Since 12th Street is a one-way street traveling north, you must access the park from Byrd Street. A parking lot for canal visitors is open from 9am-5pm, but it is always full during the week.

Bronze plaques near the parking lot explain how the locks functioned. Walk down to the river and west through the old power plant. Water rushes through the old waterworks below gratings. Inside the plant is the remains of a 90-foot packet boat unearthed when the CSX James River Center was excavated in 1983.

There have been mills on this site since 1777. Richmond grew as a manufacturing center because the drop of the James River falls could provide power for flour, cotton, paper and iron mills.

The walk continues along Haxall Canal, under the Manchester Bridge to Brown's Island. Here the path divides. One branch follows the river, the other continues along the canal. The river path leads to a pier-like observation deck stretching way out into the middle of the river. This is a thrilling walk, made even more exciting for children by the frequent trains crossing the trestle directly overhead.

The path continues to the end of Brown's Island, a popular location for festivals and concerts. The old Tredegar Iron Works can be seen in the distance and a bridge crosses the canal here if you want to continue walking in that direction. At Tredegar, waterwheels once powered machinery that made gun barrels, cannon and rolled armor for the Ironclads of the Confederacy. Later, electricity for street cars and street lights was produced there. The ruins are being partially restored.

NOTE: The park and Brown's Island are currently closed for renovation and restoration, and are scheduled to reopen in the fall of 1998.

Kanawha Place 7th and Canal Streets. An island oasis featuring a beautiful fountain and park benches. This spot is the site of "Fridays at Sunset Jazz Concert Series." Free concerts are held every night throughout the summer.

Publications available on Canal History:

The Falls of the James Atlas - $8 + $2 postage.
Guide to the Works of the James River and Kanawha Co. (from the City of Richmond to the Ohio River) - $5 + $2 postage.

For publications, contact Richard A. Davis, VC & NS Sales, Route 2, Box 254, Lexington, Va. 24450.

For additional information on Richmond's canals and locks, call William Trout, President, Richmond District of Virginia Canals & Navigations Society 288-1334.

Festival Park 6th Street Marketplace and the Coliseum. Free concerts and festivals. Call Downtown Presents at 643-2826 for activities.

Observation Deck City Hall, 900 East Broad Street. Elevators go to an outdoor observation deck (with high safety panels) on the top of City Hall. The area is accessible any time. Vending machines provide drinks. After normal business hours and on weekends, check in with the security guard on the 9th Street side of the building.

Richmond's Landmark Theater 6 North Laurel Street. Recently restored and renovated, the Landmark Theater makes a fascinating tour stop. In addition to the lobby with its interesting fountain and mosiacs and the auditorium with its guilded dome 75 feet above the floor, the building houses an old swimming pool and bowling alley, hotel suites, and the former home of the Richmond Police Academy. Call 780-8226 for information or to schedule a tour.

Flood Wall Downtown, southside of the James River. A one-and-one-half mile paved walkway stretches from the Manchester Bridge (Semmes Avenue) to I-95. Beautiful views of river rapids, wildlife, and the city skyline. Most of the trail is wheelchair accessible.

Fan

Lombardy Triangle intersection of Lombardy and Park Avenues. Toddler playground, sandbox, climbing apparatus, garden and shade trees, enclosed by a brick wall.

Meadow Street Triangle intersection of Meadow Street and Park Avenue. Small lawn and sandbox, rose garden and bronze monument to the First Virginia Infantry Regiment, all enclosed by a wrought iron fence.

Monroe Park city block, corner of Belvidere and Main Street. Large, old shade trees and many flowering trees. Firm paths radiating around a fountain. Nice for strolling. Park on Main Street near playground equipment.

Paradise Park 1700 block Grove Avenue. Toddler playground and horseshoe pits.

Scuffletown Park 2300 block Park Avenue. Toddler playground and seating. Enter through alleys on Strawberry or Stafford Streets.

East Side

Jefferson Hill Park 21st Street and East Clay Street. Beautiful overlook of the western part of the city and Shockoe Valley. Toddler playground, shaded lawns, cool breezes in summer and an old band shell. A plaque commemorating the tragic October 2, 1925, cave-in that buried a steam train and its occupants is located at the tunnel's sealed entrance off 18th Street. Park your car on Clay or Jefferson Avenue.

Taylor's Hill Park 23rd and East Grace Street, where Grace Street dead-ends. This park, most of which is on a steep slope, affords a spectacular view of the city skyline. A plaque points out landmarks. A steep trail to the left winds around the old Monte Maria Convent, now called Richmond Hill, an interdenominational retreat center, to a flat, grassy area at 21st and Franklin.

Libby Hill Park 28th and East Franklin Street. Another fantastic view of the city and the bend of the James River. Driving east on Main Street one cannot fail to see the 70-foot high Confederate Soldiers and Sailors Monument that dominates the park. An old, enclosed gazebo is used as a meeting place and is warmed by a wood-burning stove in the wintertime. Shady lawns, old oak trees.

Powhatan Hill Just beyond the curve of Williamsburg Road and Hatcher Street, take a right on Northampton Street to Goddin and park at the community center.

One of the most historic sites in North America, this is where Captain John Smith met Indian Chief Powhatan, father of Pocahontas, on May 23, 1607. The hilltop affords a view of the city. A walk to the bottom of the hill takes you to a plaque commemorating the historic meeting.

Activities are offered at the recreation center, and there are ball fields, a playground, and a swimming pool.

Chimborazo Park East Broad and 32nd Street. The National Battlefield Park Visitors Center is located here on the site where once stood the Chimborazo Field Hospital. Nearly 76,000 patients were treated here during the Civil War.

This is the headquarters of the Battlefield Park System. Exhibits and a 10-minute orientation film explain the 1861-1865 defense of Richmond. Maps and an auto tape tour of the nine area battlefields are available in the small gift shop. There are also a great many books dealing with the Civil War, some about Virginia, some children's activity books and a few souvenirs. Center open 9am-5pm.

Open play fields and picnic tables surround the Visitors Center. The hilltop park overlooks the river and tobacco warehouses. The Parcourse Fitness Cluster is designed especially for the disabled. Restrooms in the center. For more information, call 226-1981.

Gillies Creek Park Stony Run Drive and Williamsburg Road. 35-acre park with the area's only disc golf course. Eight regulation horseshoe pits, soccer field, and a lighted baseball field. Future amenities will include a BMX bike trail and regulation croquet course.

Northeast

Pine Camp 4901 Old Brook Road, one block east of Chamberlayne Avenue. Playground, picnic areas, 1.5-mile fitness trail and other trails for walking and jogging. Nature trail along Horse Swamp Creek. Baseball and soccer fields. Basketball courts. Community center with arts, crafts, dance classes, small theater and art gallery. Call 780-4322 for information.

Parks and Preserves

Highland Park Plaza Pollack Street and First Avenue. Playground, sandboxes, shaded benches, tennis courts, and horseshoe pits. Accessible to handicapped.

Pollard Park Chamberlayne Avenue and Brookland Park Boulevard. Picnicking under shade and in old gazebo. Jogging and walking trails.

Hotchkiss Field 701 East Brookland Park Boulevard. Tennis, basketball courts and hoseshoe pits. Swimming pool and community center are also featured.

Abner Clay Park Brook Road and Leigh Street. Toddler playground, tennis court, lighted ball field, small plaza for sitting and large grassy play area.

Travelland Robin Hood and Hermitage Roads. Richmond's Tourist Information Center, 358-5511. Full-sized exhibits of various modes of travel (train, plane) are on the grounds, and children are welcome to climb and explore. Small gift shop.

Battery Park Overbrook Road two blocks east of Chamberlayne Avenue. Steep slopes planted with flowering trees and shrubs; granite walkways. Once the site of the Civil War gun batteries. Playground, tennis courts, swimming pool and community center.

Bryan Park near the intersection of I-95 and I-64, enter off Lakeside Avenue. Small lake and fountain surrounded by rolling hills and woods covering 260 acres on the North Side. Azalea gardens featuring 55 varieties cover 17 acres of the park and back in 1971 drew more than 400,000 tourists. Thanks to the Friends of Bryan Park and with the blooming dogwoods, the park is a unique and spectacular sight in the spring. Tennis court, fishing, ducks to feed at the lake, many trails for biking, jogging and walking. Sledding in the wintertime. Generally accessible to wheelchairs.

Nature walk to creek and through marshy area good for sighting birds and small forest animals. Open fields for play and shady picnic areas.

Bikefest—the Friends of Bryan Park and Richmond Department of Recreation and Parks sponsor this event in spring after the azaleas start blooming. Kids and adults bike through the more than two miles of winding roads which are closed to automobile traffic. Minor bike repairs, face painting and food are also featured. Plans are currently under way for a new soccer complex with six fields. The Central Virginia Soccer Association is raising the funds. Call 780-6175 for details.

City Parks South of the James

Forest Hill Park along Forest Hill Avenue between 34th and 42nd Street. Parking off 42nd Street. This hilly, forested park was the site of the Forest Hill Amusement Park in the early 1920's and the end of the Forest Hill Streetcar Line. Once a popular promenade, the park is still a neighborhood gathering place for sledding in wintertime, with bonfires provided by the city, and kite flying and viewing recently restored azalea gardens in the spring.

The Westover Azalea Festival in April brings out hundreds of people in '20's-era costumes for a parade from George Wythe High School to the park for a day of family activities. Watch newspapers for the date.

Trails in the upper elevations of the park near the parking lot and gardens are suitable for bicycling, strollers and wheelchairs. Tables in Shelter #1 accommodate wheelchairs, as do nearby restrooms.

Tennis courts and more parking are near the Old Stone House, built in 1836. Once a penny arcade for the Forest Hill Amusement Park, the Old Stone House later became the first Southside branch of the city library and is now available for meetings.

A steep, uneven trail leads from the parking lot to the lake. Follow the trail around the lake and along Reedy Creek to the north through a deep ravine, eventually leading to Riverside Drive. During dry weather you can walk through a culvert under the road to connect with the Buttermilk Trail in the Main Section of the James River Park. This makes for a pleasant, though rugged, hike or jog.

Powhite Park 6800 block Jahnke Road, across from Chippenham Hospital (turn right on Hiokes Road into parking lot). A cool, natural area tucked between busy streets and shopping centers. Trails lead to the pond created by beavers damming up Powhite Creek. Blueberries on high ground in late summer. A few picnic tables. Plans call for a boardwalk through the marsh, more parking and restrooms.

Pocosham Park borders Chippenham Parkway south of Hull Street. Basketball court near parking lot. To get there, traveling west on Walmsley Road, turn left on Hey Road, left again on Pocosham Drive, and right on Templeton Road to parking.

Carter Jones Park Perry Street. Fonticello Spring is here, so bring containers to fill up. Picnic and play area, lighted tennis and basketball courts, ball fields, horseshoe pit and paved paths for strollers and wheelchairs. East on Semmes Avenue, right on 29th Street to Perry.

James River Park System These natural, wooded areas provide many opportunities for families to enjoy the river and the outdoors without driving long distances. Hike along the shoreline; splash in the river; explore trails through meadows, forest and marshland; hunt for wildflowers and wildlife; have a picnic; or go canoeing, rafting, tubing or fishing. The seven sections, open year-round dawn to dusk, are the Main Section, Pony Pasture, Belle Isle, Huguenot Woods, North Bank, Wetlands and Ancarrow's Landing, also known as the City Boat Ramp.

River Safety: Three Rules
1. Stay out of the river when the water level is over four feet. After a lot of rain the current can be strong. Plan to take children to the park during long dry spells. Call 649-9116 for daily water level recording.
2. Everyone should wear shoes, in and out of the water, to protect feet from glass and sharp rocks.

3. Children and non-swimmers should wear life jackets. Small children should be fitted into the type of jacket with a crotch strap to prevent it from slipping over the head.

Visitor Center Main Section, Riverside Drive, near Hillcrest 780-5311. Inside are animal displays and insect houses, maps and trail guides, nature notes, bird and wildflower guides and self-guiding tours. A volunteer on duty can answer your questions or head you in the direction of your interests. A broad range of workshops (announced in local papers) are offered here. The center is usually open Saturday mornings and sometimes during the week.

If you can't stop by the center when it is open, you can call and have maps and nature guides mailed to you. Though maps are posted near parking areas, it is difficult to find your way down trails without a map in hand.

Getting to the center (accessible on foot only) can be an adventure in and of itself. The quickest way is to park on Riverside Drive near Hillcrest Road and enter the park at the white-water boat entry sign. Follow this trail to the center. Restrooms located here are open only when the center is open.

Main Section Riverside Drive between Boulevard and Lee Bridges. Park at the 42nd Street parking area and follow trails to the Netherwood Quarry. Beyond the quarry the trail crosses a high pedestrian bridge over the railroad tracks. The trail then continues to the right, to the Visitor Center. Or hop stepping-stones across a small stream to a narrow island and the main body of the river beyond.

Pony Pasture Riverside Drive two miles east of Huguenot Bridge. Several trails begin at the parking lot just west of Rockfalls Drive. Along the shoreline are large boulders, potholes and shallow pools to explore. Watch out for mossy, slippery rocks! During the hottest part of the day children will enjoy hunting for small water creatures in the shallows. A child with a face mask on can lie face down in the water and look at big flat rocks that have water rushing over them. Looking into crevices and holes will reveal minnows and crawdads. There are many good places for this at the Pony Pasture—or anywhere that there is shallow (6 inches), fast-moving water.

The Pleasant Creek trail leads to a marshland observation point that is considered to be one of the best bird-watching locations in the city.

Look for quail, great blue heron and turkey vultures. There is a birding guide at the Visitor Center. A shorter trail to the observation deck begins at the parking area at the end of Landria Drive.

There is excellent fishing at the Pony Pasture in the mornings and evenings. Try small minnows for bass and chicken liver for catfish. The place for tubing on the James is between the Pony Pasture and the Visitor Center. This is also an easy white-water canoe run.

A scenic bicycle route begins at Scottview Drive and follows Riverside west to Huguenot Bridge.

Restrooms at the Pony Pasture parking lot are open from March to freezing weather in the fall.

Belle Isle directly under the Lee Bridge. Entrance to the park is now from the northside of the river on Tredegar Street. Park by the pylons of the Lee Bridge, then walk or take your bicycles across the suspension bridge under the Lee Bridge.

During the Civil War there was an infamous prison on this island. Still here are the ruins of an iron mill, a power plant and gun emplacements. Some of these old structures are interesting to look around, but are not safe to climb on. The old quarry is now a pond with a floating fishing dock stocked with catfish.

Children ages 9-12 years will love Passages Adventure Camp, held early June through mid-August, featuring activities such as rock climbing, rappeling, canoeing and kayaking. Call 358-0577 for information.

A self-guided Geology Walk begins at the 22nd Street parking lot and follows the shore on the mainland opposite Belle Isle. The brochure describes how the Falls of the James were formed millions of years ago in lay terms that make the process easy to visualize. There are also hands-on activities that stimulate curiosity about geological formations along the way. This tour is probably of most interest to ages 9 and older.

Huguenot Woods underneath Huguenot Bridge. The old Westham Bridge abutment can be used as a ramp accessible to wheelchairs to overlook the river. Trails meander along the shoreline. Bank fish with worms for bream and chicken livers for catfish. Bike from here to the Pony Pasture. Flat-water canoeists launch here. (See Canoeing—especially caution about the treacherous Williams Dam.)

North Bank Park at the end of Texas Avenue. Visitors can cross over the train tracks and the canal on a pedestrian bridge to picnic or fish at the river's edge. This area is not well-policed or as clean as other areas of the parks.

Hanover County

Hanover Wayside Park Off Hanover Courthouse Road (Route 301), five miles south of Hanover Courthouse. This park features 36 acres of park land, a picnic shelter, tables, grill pits, ball field, a tot-lot and a 6-acre pond. Hanover Wayside is open throughout the year. For group reservations contact the department at 798-8062. Shelter fees are $25 for residents and $35 for non-residents.

Poor Farm Park 4 miles west of Ashland off West Patrick Henry Road (Route 54); adjacent to and behind Patrick Henry High and Liberty Middle schools. Poor Farm has 205 acres of passive park with nature trails and a picnic area. Features include picnic shelters, mountain bike trails, a tot-lot, an archery range, horseshoe pits, beach volleyball courts, open play areas and an amphitheater. For group reservations contact the department. Shelter fees are $25 for residents and $35 for non-residents. Poor Farm Park now contains an 8-station orienteering course. Persons or groups may contact the department to obtain map and information on the course.

North Anna Battlefield Park on Route 684, adjacent to the General Crushed Stone Quarry. General Crushed Stone owns this 75-acre property and has granted the county an easement. Trench works with rifle pits from the Battle of North Anna are located on this property and are considered some of the most pristine examples of Civil War earthworks in existence. This passive park is comprised of an interpretive trail system and is available to the public by appointment only. For reservations, contact the department at 798-8062.

Cold Harbor Battlefield Park/Garthright House Cold Harbor Road on Route 156, four miles south of Mechanicsville business district. This 50-acre park surrounds the historically significant Garthright House.

Included on the property are numerous Civil War trenches and rifle pits. The park features a passive trail system with interpretive signs explaining historical events which occurred in the area during the Civil War.

Hanover Courthouse Park Hanover Courthouse Road (Route 301), approx. 1 mile south of Hanover Courthouse. Soccer/athletic fields, concession stand, walking/jogging track. Small boat/canoe launch sites:

> Hanover Courthouse Road/Pamunkey River - approximately 2 miles north of Hanover Courthouse on Rt. 301.
>
> Route 54/South Anna River - approximately 1 mile west of Patrick Henry High School on West Patrick Henry Road (Route 54).

Henrico County

Belmont Park 1600 Hilliard Road 262-4728. Eight tennis courts, a recreation center for numerous classes and meetings, and an 18-hole championship golf course that was the site of the 1949 PGA Championship, all on 117 acres.

Central Gardens Recreation Area 2210 Cleary Drive. Play equipment plus basketball and baseball fields.

Cheswick Park Forest Avenue between Three Chopt and Skipwith Roads. This is Henrico's oldest neighborhood park featuring the county's largest playground area. Picnic areas and tables, hiking, exercise and nature trails spread out amidst the 24-acre park.

Confederate Hills Recreation Center 302 Lee Avenue, Highland Springs 737-2859. Henrico's newest facility sits on a 5-acre site and offers a wide range of recreation classes for all age groups, as well as being available for private rentals. The site contains four tennis courts, shuffleboard and croquet courts as well.

Crump Park 3400 Mountain Road 672-5520. Spacious 150-acre park and the Meadow Farm Museum. Three miles of hiking trails with self-guiding nature trails (brochures at museum), stocked ponds, ducks to feed and fishing, playground, open fields for kite flying, horseshoe pits, picnic area, restrooms and picnic shelters for groups. For information on the many year-round activities going on, see Meadow Farm Museum.

Deep Bottom Park 9525 Deep Bottom Road. Public access to the James River with a boat landing and canoe launch. Picnic tables, grills and pier fishing. Watch small children closely.

Deep Run Park 9900 Ridgefield Parkway. Exercise, walking and bicycle trails, basketball courts, soccer and football fields, playgrounds and picnic areas on 2-acre lake. A nature pavilion and new trails have recently been added to this 167-acre park.

Dorey Park 2999 Darbytown Road 795-2334. A 400-acre park with exercise/hiking trails, tennis courts, ball fields, an equestrian ring, playgrounds, a 4-acre pond for fishing, picnic tables and group picnic facilities to accommodate up to 200 people. A recreation center is also here, located in a renovated dairy barn.

Dunncroft/Castle Point Park 4901 Francistown Road. This neighborhood park features a picnic area and tables with a play area.

Echo Lake Park 5701 Springfield Road. This 24-acre park features an 8-acre lake for fishing surrounded by 2 miles of hiking trails, picnic areas and playgrounds, restrooms and picnic shelter.

Glen Allen Softball Complex 2175 Mountain Road. This 12-acre park is a softball haven for players and fans alike.

Glen Echo Recreation Area 3808 Nine Mile Road. Tennis courts, baseball and play equipment are featured at this neighborhood park.

Hidden Creek Park 2415 Brockway Lane. A 7-acre community park with a walking trail, playground and picnic shelter. Site of the Shuttle Challenger Memorial Garden.

Parks and Preserves

Highland Springs Recreation Area 195 Ivy Street. Baseball, softball, playground equipment, picnic shelter, gazebo and a concession area are offered here.

Klehr Field 8000 Diane Lane. It's ball fields galore at this 20-acre athletic facility.

Laurel Skate Park 10301 Hungary Spring Road, 67-BOARD. Skateboard and skate fans will love this park, the only facility of its kind in central Virginia. It features a freestyle skate area, a street skate area, a half-pipe and a combination bowl. Available Monday-Friday 3pm-8pm, Saturday 10am-6pm and Sunday noon-6pm.

McGeorge Field 8081 Recreation Road. A recreation center, picnic area with tables, numerous ball fields and a concession stand are featured here.

Osborne Boat Landing 9680 Osborne Turnpike. You can fish here or launch a boat at this premier access point for the James River.

RF&P Park 3400 Mountain Road. Baseball, softball and volleyball games are the norm here, next to Crump Park.

Robinson Park 214 Westover Avenue, in Bungalow City community, off Nine Mile Road just west of Highland Springs. Basketball court, ball field, horseshoe pits, playground, picnic tables, shelter and a "For Kid's Sake" tot-lot.

Sandston Recreation Area 11 J.B. Finley Street. Ball fields and tennis are featured here.

Short Pump Park 3401 Pump Road. This 15-acre park features ball fields, playgrounds, trails and picnic tables, a shelter and restrooms adjacent to Short Pump Elementary School. A 2-room schoolhouse was recently relocated here and is currently undergoing renovation.

Springfield Park 4600 Springfield Road. Picnic tables and areas plus playground equipment for this neighborhood park adjacent to the new Springfield Park Elementary School.

Three Lakes Park 400 Sausiluta Drive. This is one of the area's most exciting parks with a nature center, aquarium, trails and more. You can even fish in two of the three lakes, and your children can take classes at the center.

Vawter Street Park/Glen Lea Recreation Area 4501 Vawter Street. Playground, ball fields, hiking, fitness and nature trails, picnic shelter and restrooms.

Virginia Randolph Recreation Area 2206 Mountain Road. You can enjoy softball, football, soccer, basketball and tennis at this community park.

Chesterfield County

Appomattox River Canoe Landing 21400 Chesdin Road. This 5-acre park offers a picnic area, fishing and river access with a car-top boat launch.

Bensley Park 2900 Drewry's Bluff Road. Picnic areas, playground equipment, a concession stand, tennis courts and ball fields can be found here amidst the 30 acres. Community building available for rental. Phone 748-1126.

Bird Athletic Complex 10301 Courthouse Road. Picnic areas, playground equipment, a concession stand, tennis courts and ball fields can be found here amidst the 30 acres.

Clarendon Park 2428 Brookforest Road. There is a picnic area and playground equipment here with self-guided trails in the process of being designed.

Clover Hill Athletic Complex 3300 Mount Herman Road. This 109-acre park with two ballfields opened in 1996.

Coalfield Soccer Complex 1700 Miners Trail Road. This 34-acre athletic complex features a well-used soccer field.

Courthouse Athletic Complex 6804 West Krause Road. Volleyball, baseball and softball fields take up much of this 4-acre athletic complex.

Davis Athletic Complex 415 South Providence Road. Baseball and soccer fields are available here.

Dutch Gap Boat Launch 501 Coxendale Road. This 10-acre park offers a picnic area, fishing and river access with a boat ramp.

Eppington Plantation Historical Park 14600 Eppes Falls Road 748-1623. This historical park features a picnic area. The plantation can be toured by appointment.

Ettrick Park 20400 Laurel Road, 526-5596 or 748-1623. This 24-acre park has something for everyone with a picnic area, playground equipment, horseshoes, volleyball, tennis and ball fields plus a concession stand and restrooms. A community building is also available for rental.

Ettrick Riverside Park 21601 Chesterfield Avenue. A small picnic area plus historical significance makes this tiny park very special.

Fernbrook Park 4400 Fordham Place. Tennis courts plus a picnic area can be found at this 4-acre park neighborhood park located along Horner's Run Creek.

Fort Stevens Historical Park 8920 Pam Avenue. This 2-acre park features a picnic area and a self-guided tour.

Goyne Park 5300 Ecoff Road. This 33-acre park has something for everyone with tennis courts, baseball, football and soccer fields. Picnic shelters and a children's play area overlook Great Branch Creek. Trail throughout the park, through woodland and by creek.

Greenfield Athletic Complex 10751 Savoy Road. Soccer and baseball fields take up the 6-acre athletic complex.

Harrowgate Park 4200 Cougar Trail. This 29-acre park has something for everyone with a picnic area, playground equipment, horseshoes, volleyball, tennis courts and ball fields plus a concession stand and restrooms.

Henricus Historical Park 601 Coxendale Road. Beginning at the boat landing, there is a 1.5-mile trail following the James River, crossing the old river channel and becoming an 800-foot marsh boardwalk. Eventually the trail approaches a steep bluff with a spectacular view of the river.

The interpretive signs at the overlook shelter tell the history of the park, the site of the second English settlement in Virginia (1611). Monuments mark the sites of the first Episcopal Parish in Virginia, the first university in North America, and Mount Malada, North America's first hospital. The town was wiped out by an Indian massacre in 1622.

Before visiting the park, obtain the Henricus Historical Park brochure at Richmond Visitor Centers. This brochure gives a lengthy and colorful history of Henricus.

Huguenot Park 10901 Robious Road. Pine and hardwood trees provide cover for songbirds and small animals. Life Course fitness trail connects with other trails suitable for walking or jogging, wheelchairs, strollers, bicycles. Interpretive signs mark trees, shrubs and azalea gardens.

Shady playground with picnic tables within site near the Robious Road entrance. Restrooms accessible to handicapped. Group picnic shelters, tennis and basketball courts, soccer and a signed bicycle route that extends into surrounding neighborhoods.

Iron Bridge Park 6600 White Pine Road. The largest of the county's parks at 367 acres with nature trails and bike trail for scouting wildlife; a one-mile jogging trail; and a ¼-mile paved trail with exercise equipment adapted for use by handicapped. Baseball, soccer and football fields as well as handball, racquet ball and basketball courts are available. A playground, picnic shelters and restrooms can also be found.

Matoaca Park 1900 Halloway Avenue. A 43-acre park with lighted tennis courts and basketball courts and baseball, softball and football fields. Picnic areas and shelter, playgrounds and restrooms. Pine and hardwood forests to explore on a nature trail.

Point of Rocks Park 201 Enon Church Road. A system of trails provides access to the lower part of the 188-acre park. Pick up the Ashton Creek Trail self-guided tour at the Homestead Interpretive Center, an old log cabin at the beginning point of all trails. Arrowheads, artifacts from colonial and Civil War times and natural history displays are in the center.

There is a mile-long boardwalk through freshwater tidal marshland and an observation tower and blind for observing birds and other animals. Among wildlife to be seen in the park are deer, fox, wild turkey and beaver. Birds are attracted by the plantings near the bird blind.

Quartzite, which Indians collected for making arrowheads, can be seen in Cobblestone Creek.

To take part in the interpretive programs occasionally offered by county naturalists call 674-1629 or check the Parks and Recreation activities schedule. Athletic facilities here include tennis and basketball courts, football, baseball and soccer fields. Picnic shelters, playgrounds and restrooms are also available.

Rockwood Park corner of Route 360 and Courthouse Road 748-1623. Playgrounds and four picnic shelters, nature trails and nature center, baseball fields, tennis and basketball courts and a large archery range. Exercise stations along a firm trail suitable for wheelchairs. Handicapped restrooms. Concessions. Garden plots for rent April-November, $20 to $30 per season.

Self-guided tours of the Gregory's Pond Trail at the nature center behind the athletic fields. Almost four miles of trails wind through an oak/hickory forest, along the pond, following the creek through a swamp and past an 18th-century grist mill.

White-tailed deer and beaver live in the forest—you might catch a glimpse of their gnawing. Many birds, such as the great blue heron, osprey and nuthatch also live here.

Rockwood Park Nature Center (674-1629) In a cozy cabin in the woods behind the ball fields, children learn about the park's ecosystems and inhabitants. Come face-to-face with turtles. See and learn about some common snakes. Search for animals hiding in the pond. Solve the puzzles and games at the Children's Corner. You can even test your nature knowledge at the Nature Jeopardy Board!

Naturalist-conducted history/environmental activities for groups are available upon request. Activities may be designed to supplement school science, language, social studies, arts and math curricula, or develop a program with the naturalist's help to suit your group's interests. For example: build a bird house, explore trails at night, study an aquatic community or an endangered species, or learn Native American skills and games. Pick your own location from Chesterfield's parks. The Nature Center is open Saturdays and Sundays, noon to 5pm beginning April 19.

Warbro Athletic Complex in the northern area of Chesterfield County. This complex composed of 72 acres has three lighted ball fields with associated parking lots. A restroom/concession facility is under construction and should be open in the spring of 1997.

Chester Linear Park is a 1-mile-long walking trail located in central Chesterfield County. This trail is built upon an old railroad bed and has a nicely landscaped sitting area with benches.

State Parks and Preserves in Central Virginia

Virginia State Parks are designed to offer a full range of outdoor family activities in a safe and natural setting. Among these activities are fishing, boating, swimming, hiking, riding and bicycling. Camping is offered in 19 of the 28 parks.

Visitor centers, boat launching, beaches, pools, bath houses, boat rentals and other concessions generally operate from Memorial Day to Labor Day. Annual parking and swimming passes are available and offer the frequent State Park visitor a substantial savings. Appropriate fishing licenses are required.

Many parks offer environmental education programs for groups of children. Programs can be pre-arranged and tailored toward a particular group's interests. Contact individual park offices for more information.

Outdoor adventure programs are available throughout the year at most State Parks.

To reserve a cabin or campsite or to receive more information, call the Virginia State Park Reservation Center at 1-800-933-PARK. In the Richmond area call 225-3867 (TDD, 786-2121).

There are 1,313 campsites in 19 different parks, including primitive, standard, water and electric hook-up, and group sites.

The following parks are within about an hour's drive of Richmond.

Bear Creek Lake State Park Cumberland, VA 492-4410. West of Richmond in the heart of the Cumberland State Forest, Bear Creek Lake offers day visiting and overnight camping. There is a sandy swimming beach with a lifeguard, bathhouse and concessions. Canoe and paddleboat rentals, and fishing on the lake. Picnic area with grills, shelters and restrooms. Hiking trails across gentle, rolling hills and through mixed forest, plus access to Cumberland State Forest trails. Campgrounds with restrooms, showers and trailer dump station. Fees for camping and boat rentals, day visitor parking, and swimming.

Chippokes Plantation State Park Surry, VA (757) 294-3625. Located off State Route 10, directly across the James River from Jamestown, Chippokes Plantation in Surry County has been a working farm for more than 360 years. Part of the first permanent English colony, the farm offers a spectacular view of the James River and its bluffs. Visitors may tour the antebellum mansion, stroll through formal gardens or view a collection of antique farm and forestry equipment in the Farm and Forestry Museum. Visitor Center displays and audiovisual programs explain the history of agriculture from 1619 to the present. The annual Pork, Pine and Peanut Festival is held at Chippokes the third full weekend in July. New in 1997, a campground will be opened for visitors. There are also seasonal family canoe tours offered.

The park is open all year in good weather with no entrance fee. There is a small fee for parking and entrance to the mansion. Fees for swimming pool and bicycle rental. Restrooms with wheelchair access. Vending machines.

Holliday Lake State Park Appomattox, VA 248-6308. Just minutes from the famous Appomattox National Historical Park, Holliday Lake offers a scenic 150-acre lake amid rolling hills. Activities include fishing, boat and sailboat rentals, swimming and picnicking. The park offers shaded campsites and miles of lakefront hiking trails.

Lake Anna State Park Spotsylvania, VA (540) 854-5503. This park offers public access to Lake Anna, the fourth largest lake in Virginia. Recreational opportunities include waterskiing, sailing and fishing for large-mouth and striped bass, crappie and pickerel. Seasonal programs here include "panning for gold."

Visitor Center exhibits recount gold and iron mining which once took place in the area. Interpretive programs are available upon request. There are self-guided nature trails along the shore of the lake. Picnic tables and restrooms.

Nominal fee for parking and boat launching ramp. Day use only.

Pocahontas State Park and State Forest Chesterfield, VA 796-4255. Located just four miles from Chesterfield County Courthouse and 20 miles from downtown Richmond, Pocahontas State Park offers a lot of opportunities for outdoor family fun. Day use activities include picnicking, swimming in a large pool, playgrounds, paddleboat and rowboat rental and fishing.

Self-guided nature walks, as well as those led by park interpreters in the summer and on spring and fall weekends, take advantage of the park's proximity to the state forest and Swift Creek Lake, which forms the nucleus of the park. Diversity of plant and animal species is encouraged by forest management in action, and many stages of forest growth can be observed.

Bring a bike for the 3.5-mile Grist Mill Trail, through woods and clearings to the old mill.

The Awareness Trail and the Visitor Center, as well as restrooms at the center and picnic shelter #2 are designed for use by the handicapped in wheelchairs.

Hiking and horseback riding are allowed in designated areas. Call Park Headquarters for information and maps.

Camping and cabin reservations should be made by calling the Virginia State Parks Reservation Center, weekdays from 9am to 4pm, at (800)

933-PARK. Cabins can be reserved for groups, but you may have to call up to a year in advance. You can call the same number for a brochure that lists current fees and reservation information for every park in the state.

Schedules of natural history programs and maps are available at the park office, or contact the park manager.

Twin Lakes State Park Green Bay, VA 392-3435. Located five miles southwest of Burkeville, off State Route 613, the park's two lakes offer swimming, boating and fishing. Other park activities include picnicking, hiking, biking and tent camping. Cabins can be rented in summer and winter months. There are fees for parking, camping, swimming, paddleboat and rowboat rentals. Cedar Crest Conference Center is available for family reunions, business and training meetings and wedding receptions.

York River State Park Croaker, VA (757) 566-3036, (757) 566-8523. The York River is part of a large estuarine system created by mixing of fresh and salt water. A slide presentation and "hands-on" displays at the Visitor Center explain the complexities of the ever-changing environment of the estuary and marshland. Groups and families can make reservations for a fascinating canoe trip on the Taskinas Creek, which winds its way through marsh grasses. The two- to three-hour trip usually takes place in the afternoon and evening.

A series of programs for children and adults are offered by park personnel in the summertime. Past seasons have included demonstrations on cleaning and cooking crabs, followed by tasting, as well as nighttime hikes.

There is a self-guided nature trail along the river, which connects with a gravel biking/hiking trail. There are numerous fitness stations along the way. A variety of birds, flowers, trees and other wildlife can be encountered along the 20 miles of trails.

Other activities include saltwater fishing and crabbing . There are picnic tables, shelters and a playground. Modest fee for parking and canoe trips. Day use only.

Wildlife Preserves and Other Natural Areas

Chesapeake Corporation Nature Trail Over 500 acres of woodland owned by the Chesapeake Corp. with miles of nature trail well described by a self-guiding brochure. Pick up the brochure at the box at the beginning of the trail. Three lengths of trail are available, ranging from 0.8 to 3.5 miles. Day hiking only. No facilities. Watch out for poison ivy.

Harrison Lake National Fish Hatchery 829-2421. A small visitor/environmental education center with aquarium and exhibits on fish and wildlife, open April 1-October 31. The hatchery propagates striped bass, American shad and Atlantic sturgeon for stocking tributaries of the Chesapeake Bay and James River. Hatchery ponds are not interpreted unless arrangements are made in advance for tour, talk and slide show presented by staff.

A nature trail follows Herring Creek and a bird-watching platform overlooks a pond at the edge of the woods. Center and restrooms accessible to those in wheelchairs, but trail is too narrow for easy access; handicapped accessible fishing piers on a public fishing lake are also available. Center hours vary, so call ahead.

Chickahominy Wildlife Management Area 829-5336. Old gravel roads used as hiking and horseback trails access the 5,300 acres of tidal marshes, swamps, beaver ponds, creeks and some upland forest along the Chickahominy River where it joins the James River. Lots of wildlife to be seen, including the poisonous copperhead snake (wear boots). Blue herons breed in tall swamp trees, and bald eagles have been sighted near Morris Creek.

There is a boat ramp on the creek two miles north of where the creek runs into the Chickahominy River and a canoe launch at the bridge on Route 623 for a 4-mile downstream trip to the boat ramp. Fishing is very good here, and wildlife is easily spotted from boats.

Restrooms and drinking water at Mt. Zion Park across Route 623. Scout troops may camp here but must prearrange with the WMA office. Hunting is allowed here in season, so call the WMA to find out when to stay clear of hunters.

Powhatan Wildlife Management Area 598-4286. Miles of trails for hiking and horseback riding through 4,200 acres of rolling Piedmont hills. Lakes, streams, meadows and forests are the habitats of wildlife, birds and flowers. Good fishing.

Call the field office for maps showing trails, boat ramps and parking lots and to avoid the hunting season. No restrooms or drinking water. Scouts may camp by making arrangements with wildlife area manager.

Powhatan County along Route 60, about five miles west of Powhatan County Courthouse. Eight access roads from Route 60 leading to parking lots. Look for Game Commission signs.

Presquile National Wildlife Refuge 733-8042. An island refuge on the James River for thousands of wintering-over waterfowl. Accessible only by refuge ferry, on a reservation basis. Interpretive brochures available at Visitor Center describe the ¾-mile trail through the woods, tidal marsh and swamp. Old farm fields planted with wheat, corn, clover and fescue provide grazing for thousands of Canadian geese in fall and winter. Hundreds of ducks winter on the island.

A bird list is also available at the center. Bald eagles are commonly seen, as are wild turkeys in morning and afternoon. Other wildlife commonly sighted are red fox, muskrat, beaver, deer and raccoon, as well as reptiles.

For a short one- or two-hour trip, a good time to take young children is during open house, held twice a year; call the refuge manager for dates. Other field trips open to the public take place throughout the year. Watch newspapers for announcements.

To arrange a group or family visit during the week call the refuge manager. Office hours vary, so call several weeks ahead of date and keep trying if no answer.

There is no fee for the ferry, which accommodates 30 and docks at the end of State Route 827. Limited wheelchair access.

For more information write Refuge Manager, Presquile National Wildlife Refuge, PO Box 189, Prince George, VA 23875.

Chapter 4

Science and Nature

> **Science Centers**
> **Places of Interest**
> **Pick-Your-Own Farms**
> **Christmas Trees**

Carolyn Pelnik, Age 6
"Flowers"

Science Centers

Science Museum of Virginia 2500 West Broad Street 367-6552. Beneath the rotunda of the 1920s Broad Street train station are fascinating hands-on exhibits and activities dealing with nature and technology. Permanent displays on crystal formation, optical illusions, aerodynamics, computers and the underwater world of the Chesapeake Bay. Changing themes have dealt with robotics, dinosaurs, aviation, calligraphy and much more.

The Ethyl Universe Theater presents OMNIMAX and IMAX films and planetarium programs.

Classes for children and families are offered continuously and deal with marine life, weather, constellations, electricity, computers—an endless number of topics.

Expeditions sponsored include canoe trips; archaeological digs; gem- and rock-hunting trips to area mines; bus trips to the National Aquarium, Street Michaels Maritime Museum and Annapolis.

Skywatch—Observe the evening sky with the Richmond Astronomical Society on the museum lawn, free. Usually the third Friday, monthly, around 8pm, weather permitting.

Museum shop carries a broad selection of scientific supplies including fossils, geodes, earth and moon globes, star finders, crystals, archaeological kits, puzzles and books reasonably priced.

Annual events such as Joy from the World (an international holiday festival in December), a spring flight festival and a harvest celebration.

Family memberships include free admission to exhibits; discounts on films and movies, classes and special events, trips and museum purchase; newsletter and calendar. Call for admission fees.

Lora Robins Gallery of Design from Nature University of Richmond 289-8237. Collections of rocks and minerals, gems and jewels, seashells and corals, fossils and cultural artifacts. You'll also find a giant, man-eating clam shell from "down under"! Specimens are displayed by scientific groupings or are combined to relate natural history to countries and cultures.

The fluorescent mineral room is the best of its kind in the country. The Lalique Lounge features carved precious metals such as jade, opal and tourmaline. Also on display will be an outstanding collection of porcelains by Edward Marshall. Of special interest to young children are the baby dinosaur fossils.

The gallery features 30-to-60-minute educational programs relating to gallery exhibits, viewed on an 8-foot television screen.

Admission to the gallery is free. Open weekdays 10am-4pm, weekends 1pm-5pm.

Lewis Ginter Botanical Garden at Bloemendaal 1800 Lakeside Avenue 262-9887. Bloemendaal, once the residence and model farm of Grace Arents, niece of tobacco baron Ginter, is now the Lewis Ginter Botanical Garden. The garden has thousands of colorful plants from around the world. The Henry M. Flagler Perennial Garden is the Garden's most extensive display, boasting 12,000 plants and 655 different cultivars across three acres of land. Plans for continued development over the next 20 years include glass-domed conservatories, reflection pools, restaurants, fountains and a trolley.

Children enjoy exploring the Children's Garden with its bright array of plants from different regions of the world. A nearby woodland features turtles, muskrats, chipmunks and many other forms of wildlife. Look for newspaper announcements of family-oriented activities such as the Rare Plant Sale in September, with puppets, barbershop quartet and frozen yogurt. "Fall for All at Bloemendaal" hosts an old-fashioned country fair with petting zoo, pumpkin decorating, agricultural displays, gold-panning, flower show and refreshments.

Children have been featured at the Lewis Ginter Botanical Garden's World Gardenfest for Children. A sampling of international flora, food and fun included a rain forest exhibit, Scottish bagpipes, flower arranging for children and the sensory exploration of the Children's Garden.

Admission fee charged. Call for hours and information about special events and classes.

Directions: North on Brook Road (Route 1), left on Hilliard, right on Lakeside. Entrance at the first drive on the left.

Maymont 1700 Hampton Street, adjacent to Byrd Park 358-7166 A not-to-be-missed experience! (see listing in Chapter 3, Parks and Preserves).

Nature Centers, see Parks

Places of Interest

Metro Richmond Zoo 8300 Beaver Bridge, Moseley 739-5666. With more than 300 animals roaming the area, this new, small zoo is Richmond's attempt to expose children and their families to animals other than those typically found on nearby farms and petting zoos that travel from mall to mall. Like big city zoos, you'll see giraffes, kangaroos, zebra, gazelle and more. You can also pet and feed some of them, too.

Open Monday through Saturday, 9am-6pm most of the year, Saturdays only in January and February. Admission charged.

Morefield Mines Amelia, VA 561-3399. One of Richmond's best-kept secrets. At this actual working mine, children and moms and dads can satisfy their desire for gems of all shapes and sizes. You can actually find garnets, topaz and much more, as well as plain old rocks, by digging into dirt and sifting it through the sluice. Most rock hounds come for the blue-green amazonite or twelve other frequently found gemstones. Best bet is to bring your own sealable sandwich bags for storing your gems, and participants should definitely wear rubber boots and work clothes that will get dirty. Call for prices and hours.

Directions: West on Route 360. Three miles before Amelia, take a left on Route 628. Go one mile and watch for signs.

Rocks, Gems, Crystals, Fossils – see Frances' Stones; Packard's Rock Shop (in Chapter 9, Hobbies); Aquarian Bookshop (in Chapter 9, Books); and Museum Shops (also Chapter 9, Museum Shops).

Springs There are two freshwater springs located within the city limits and maintained by the City of Richmond. These springs are open all year and accessible during daylight hours. Call the City of Richmond Parks and Recreation Department at 780-5733 for specifics. Bring containers.

Fonticello Spring, Carter Jones Playground, 29th and Bainbridge.
Wayside Spring, 4800 New Kent Road, seven blocks west of
 Forest Hill Park in a ravine at the intersection of Prince George.

Science and Nature

County Extension Agent Contacts County Agricultural Extension Agents are often able to arrange field trips for groups to local farms. They also provide a variety of programs and services related to farming and home economics.

Charles City, 829-9241
Chesterfield, 751-4401
Goochland, 556-5341
Hanover, 752-4310
Henrico, call 672-5160
New Kent, 966-9645
Powhatan, 598-5640 or 794-9593
Richmond City, 786-4150

Henrico Extension offers a recorded tips number at 672-5178.

"Pick-Your-Own" Farms

If you like fresh fruits and vegetables and fresh country air, there are plenty of pick-your-own farms within 50 miles of Richmond where you can pick everything from apples to zucchini. You can also buy fresh-picked. Many farms are geared especially for children's visits, providing petting zoos, hayrides and refreshments. Some also sell a variety of farm products—homemade jellies and jams and craft items.

We have included a few close-by farms and some of our favorites. A state guide to fresh produce in Virginia is available from the Virginia Department of Agriculture and Consumer Services. Call them at 786-5867 and request a copy of "Virginia Grown: A Guide to Pick-Your-Own and Fresh-Picked Produce, Honey and Retail Farmers' Markets." Or order the guide by mail at VDACS, PO Box 1163, Richmond, VA 23218. VDACS also has available the "Virginia Christmas Tree Guide," the "Virginia Food Festival Directory" and the "Virginia Specialties Gifts by Mail Catalog." Order them all when you contact VDACS.

Chesterfield County

Chesterfield Berry Farm and Market Moseley, VA 739-3831. Ride out to fields in hay wagons to pick strawberries in May and June, blackberries in mid-July and August, pumpkins in October. Apples for sale from bins in October. Lots of fun for children. Petting barn with cows, goats, sheep, pigs, rabbits, chickens and turkeys. Snacks for sale and hotdog roasting. Reservations for school groups in fall, as well as for hayrides and bonfires.

Handcraft Festival first weekend in October, and Pumpkin Festival third weekend with games, pumpkin decorating, pig-calling contest, live music and barbecued chicken dinners. Call Harvest Hotline, 739-3831, for picking conditions.

Directions: West on Route 360 about 8 miles past Brandermill. Right on Route 603, two miles, then left on Pear Orchard Road, five miles to farm.

Swift Creek Berry Farm 17210 Genito Road, Moseley, VA 739-2037. Pick-your-own and fresh-picked blueberries.

Walthall Berries and More 2020 Ruffin Mill Road, Chesterfield, VA 526-4000. Pick-your-own strawberries and pumpkins as well as fall activities, including a straw maze, hayrides to pick the pumpkins and even haunted hayrides at night. Group picnics can be arranged. Cut-your-own Christmas trees after Thanksgiving. Call ahead to confirm.

Goochland County

Maidens Thornless Blackberries Maidens, VA 556-4164. Bring your own containers to fill with juicy pick-your-own blackberries. Mid-July through August. Call before coming.

Hanover County

Ashland Berry Farm 227-3601. The pick-your-own farm was designed with children and fun in mind. Pickers take a free hayride out to the field to gather whatever is in season—strawberries, thornless blackberries, sweet corn, pumpkins. No charge for what's eaten in the fields!

Pumpkin Harvest Hayride Tour and Pumpkin Playland. Petting barn and pony rides. Greenhouse mid-April to June. Christmas Shop October-December and Christmas trees. Roast-your-own hotdogs, homemade donuts, apples, cider and peanuts along with other concessions for sale. Haunted barn and make-your-own scarecrow in October. Field trips, group hayrides and bonfires by reservation, September-November. Hours and events vary throughout the year. Call for information about children's activities.

Directions: North on I-95 to Ashland exit, west on Route 54. Turn right on Route 1, four miles, then left on Route 738 for four miles.

Graves Plant Farm Mechanicsville, VA 779-2083. Pick-your-own asparagus (mid-April), blueberries (June) and blackberries.

Hollins Hanover Honey Mechanicsville, VA 746-5773. Here's a chance to see an actual Honey House operation with an observation hive in season and beehives on site. Equipment and supplies are available plus several flavors of comb and liquid honey. Please call before visiting.

King's Pick Your Own Farm Ashland, VA 550-3189. Pick-your-own and fresh-picked produce in a wide variety are available, including more than 68 acres of vegetables. This farm grows specialty produce for many of the area's restaurants and markets.

Winfrey's Mechanicsville, VA 746-5984. Pick-your-own strawberries.

King and Queen County

Plainview Farm Plain View, VA 785-6407. Pick-your-own or fresh-picked strawberries (May 1), English peas (mid-May) and assorted vegetables throughout the summer.

King William County

Lowe's Arlington Farm King William, VA 769-2815. Pick-your-own vegetables, herbs, blueberries and other fruits. Apples may be bought at the farm.

New Kent County

Woodbourne Plantation New Kent, VA 932-3693. Five acres of pick-your-own blueberries plus swimming and recreation facilities.

Powhatan County

Powhatan Berry Farm Powhatan, VA 598-3856. Pick-your-own and fresh-picked asparagus, sour cherries, strawberries, blackberries, apples, peaches, grapes, pears, pawpaws, figs and Oriental persimmons. No toxic chemicals are used on the plants.

Spotsylvania County

Finnegan's Forest Nursery & Berry Farm Partlow, VA (540) 582-2606. Pick-your-own and fresh-picked strawberries, blueberries, blackberries and raspberries. Landscape trees, perennials and bedding plants are also available.

Snead's Asparagus Farm Fredericksburg, VA (540) 371-9328. Pick-your-own and fresh-picked strawberries. A variety of spring and summer vegetables are available (already picked) starting May 1.

Westmoreland County

Westmoreland Berry Farm 493-9050. This farm is beautifully located along the Rappahannock River in the Northern Neck Region of Virginia, with breathtaking vistas. Pick-your-own strawberries, pumpkins,

Science and Nature

blueberries, raspberries, etc. Gift baskets and already picked fruits, preserves and gifts are available also.

Christmas Trees

Ready-cut and cut-your-own trees are available at most places starting after the Thanksgiving weekend. Call for hours and specifics. Make sure to order the "Virginia Christmas Tree Guide" from the Department of Agriculture and Consumer Services mentioned at the beginning of the pick-your-own section earlier in this chapter.

Amelia County

Shady Oaks Tree Farm 561-2409. Featuring Scotch and white pine trees. Open Friday-Sunday.

Caroline County

Four Springs Christmas Tree Farm 633-9336. White, Virginia and Scotch pine trees. Open daily.

Chester County

Emerson Christmas Tree Farm 530-3002. Virginia, Scotch and white pine and Norway Spruce. Open Saturday and Sunday after Thanksgiving. Open daily from the second week of December.

Chesterfield County

Ash Grove Christmas Tree Farm 275-2204. White and Scotch pine trees. Open Thursday through Sunday.

Chesterfield Berry Farm 739-3831. White pine and red cedar trees. Saws and wrapping provided. Open daily except Wednesdays.

White Goose Farm 354-5363. White pine and Norway spruce trees. Open Friday-Sunday.

Cumberland County

Nuckols Tree Plantation Cumberland, VA 492-4144. Spruce, Scotch, Austrian and white pine trees are available. Open Friday-Monday.

Hanover County

Beaver Tree Farm 746-0372. Norway spruce, white and Scotch pine trees available. Open weekends.

Gooseberry Tree Farm 781-0456. White and Scotch pine trees are available. Open Friday through Sunday or by appointment during the week.

Hanover Pines Farm 449-6014. Scotch and white pine, Colorado blue spruce and Fraser fir trees available. They will shake the old, dead needles out of your tree for you and put it in a net for the drive home. Hayrides. Gift shop. Open Friday, Saturday and Sunday.

Santa's Forest Hanover, VA 746-0011. Cut your own trees on weekends after Thanksgiving. They provide saws to cut Scotch or white pine and Leyland Cypress trees 4- to 8-feet tall. Saturdays and Sundays.

Windy Knoll Farm Mechanicsville, VA 730-TREE. Cut-your-own and pre-cut trees available. Hand bow saws and tree nets provided; tractors and wagons go to the fields where help is available if needed. Seasonal Christmas Shop on the farm. Ball and burlap trees also available. Open the day after Thanksgiving to December 21 except Sundays.

Henrico County

Rolling Oaks Farm 270-1576. Scotch and white pine trees are available, plus fresh wreaths. Open daily after Thanksgiving.

Chapter 5

Sports

> **Spectator**
> **Participatory**
>> Bicycling, Bowling, Boating/Tubing, Canoeing, Camping, Fishing, Golf, Gymnastics, Hiking, Horseback Riding, Ice Skating & Sledding, Marathons, Roller Skating, Skiing, Swimming, Team Sports, Tennis

Lauren Taylor, Age 5
"Bicycling"

Spectator Sports

Richmond Braves Baseball The Diamond, 3001 North Boulevard 359-4444. Professional ball games played in the beautiful Diamond ballpark, home to the Atlanta Brave AAA team. Games are played April-August. The club produces a seasonal newsletter called the *Tom Tom* which is targeted to children throughout Virginia. The Diamond will also host birthday parties for children. As for the games themselves, they are covered extensively by local news channels—you may see yourself in crowd shots on the evening news with the Diamond Duck! Binoculars make it easier for young children to see, and plenty of promotional events make attending a game fun for all. A Fourth of July fireworks celebration is the perfect way to end a night at the ballpark.

Games played Monday-Saturday 7pm, Sundays 2pm, and 6pm for doubleheaders.

Richmond Coliseum 601 East Leigh Street (7th Street and Marshall), 780-4956 (taped listing of events). Hosts a wide spectrum of sporting and spectator events including Richmond Renegades hockey, college basketball, WWF wrestling, Ringling Brothers and Barnum & Bailey Circus, concerts and more.

College Teams (Call for current schedules and fees.)

University of Richmond Robins Center Ticket Office 289-8388. Division I-AA Yankee Conference football is played at the UR Stadium; all other sports are played on campus. There are no fees for swimming and wrestling, November-February; track indoors, December-March, outdoor March-May; tennis, baseball, women's basketball, lacrosse.

Virginia Commonwealth University 828-1RAM. Men's basketball, November-February at Richmond Coliseum, women's at VCU gym. Men's baseball at The Diamond, women's softball at Parker Field. Cross country, soccer, women's field hockey and volleyball August-November; swimming October-February; golf March-May.

Sports

Virginia State University Petersburg, VA 520-6442. Division II Central Intercollegiate Athletic Association football and basketball games are played on campus. There is also track and tennis. Call for prices and times.

Virginia Union University 257-5840. Division II Central Intercollegiate Athletic Association football at Hovey Field on campus; men's and women's basketball at the Arthur Ashe Center near The Diamond. Also track, tennis, wrestling and golf.

Randolph-Macon College 752-7223. Division III Old Dominion Athletic Conference football takes place on campus at Day Field. Also, college basketball as well as men's and women's soccer is on campus.

Auto Racing

Richmond International Raceway at the State Fairgrounds offers 85,000 fans from around the city and the state the chance to see NASCAR Winston Cup racing in early March and again in September. The Virginia 400 is held after Labor Day. For the many other racing events scheduled, ticket prices and general infromation, call 345-7223.

Richmond Dragway (737-1193) offers bracket and amateur racing in several classes Saturday nights from March to August, Sundays from September to November and the first and third Fridays of every month from March to November. This track is a half-mile east of Richmond International Airport on Portugee Road. Call for ticket prices. Free parking.

Southside Speedway 751-LAPS. A one-third of a mile oval delivers a NASCAR-sanctioned short-track racing program every Friday night from April through early September. Located on Genito Road two miles north of Hull Street. Call for ticket prices or more information.

Virginia Motorsports Park Dinwiddie County. Host to a variety of auto events including drag racing's Penzoil Nationals. The track is also host to some amateur and bracket races in several classes every Saturday night from March through October. Call Virginia Motorsports Park Hotline at 862-3174 for ticket prices and more information.

Golf

Richmond is host to a professional golf touring event, the **Nike Dominion Open**, held at the Dominion Club in Wyndham, located in northwestern Henrico County. The tournament is usually held in late May or early June. While outstanding professional golf has been the main attraction, especially popular, too, have been the Nike Night Concerts during the event. For more information about events and ticket availability, call the Dominion Club at 360-1200.

Ice Hockey

Richmond is host to the professional sports champion, the **Richmond Renegades**, winners of the East Coast Hockey League's Riley Cup championship in the 1994-95 season. In existence for six years now, the Renegades offer 35 home games at the Coliseum with respectable ticket prices and plenty of close-up action. Kids will marvel at the fast skating and scoring and delight in the intermission activities featuring flying souvenirs and on-ice games. Also, the Renegades offer family skating on the ice after Sunday afternoon contests. Renegades Box Office: 643-PUCK.

Soccer

In a town that features a multitude of soccer activities for children, Richmond is also the home of the **Richmond Kickers**, one of the best teams in the United Systems of Independent Soccer Leagues. The Kickers, part of the new Division II professional Soccer A League, play their games at UR Stadium. Tickets are one of the best bargains in town. The 10-game home schedule begins in April and extends into August. For more information, call 644-5425.

Tennis

Each year the **Nations Bank City Tennis Championships** run from mid-May until mid-June at the Byrd Park tennis complex with a variety of championships at all age and competitive levels. For more information call the Richmond Tennis Association at 358-7872.

State championship tennis for men and women is played in August at Raintree Swim and Racquet Club 740-0026.

Richmond is very recently home to a professional tennis tour, the **Nuveen Tour**, sponsored by Trigon. The Nuveen Tour, a premier men's 35 and over professional tennis circuit, features such players as Jimmy Connors, Yannick Noah, Andres Gomez, Johan Kriek and many others. Matches are held at Robious Sports and Fitness Center, which houses a new 3,000 seat stadium with outdoor clay courts. The tournament will be held annually in late April. Proceeds benefit the Richmond Children's Hospital. For more information, call Trigon Champions ticket office at 747-7597, toll free at (888) 299-PROS or Robious Sports and Fitness at 330-2222.

Participatory Sports

Bicycling

Registration: Henrico requires all bicycles to be registered with the Division of Police (672-4809). The license is valid for the life of the bike. No license is required in Richmond, Chesterfield or Hanover County.

Bicycling enthusiasts probably know by heart 266-BIKE, the source for bike tours, maps and other information for the Richmond area, sponsored by the Richmond Area Bicycling Association. Listed are rides, race information and results, and a fax-on-demand service for maps of the following areas: Western Henrico/Hanover County, Eastern Hanover County, South of the James, Eastern Henrico County, Riverside Drive.

Bicycling in Area Parks There are bicycle trails in these parks: Byrd, Bryan, Forest Hill, Deep Run, Huguenot, York River State Park and Twin Lakes State Park. There are trails and bike rentals in Pocahontas and Chippokes Plantation State Parks. There is also a nice ride on Riverside Drive from the Pony Pasture to Huguenot Woods.

Local Bicycle Tours The Richmond Area Bicycle Association (RABA) is the main source for any organized biking activities. Their comprehensive Adventure Line at 266-BIKE offers recorded announcements about trails, biking events, as well as faxed information of trails for the entire area. RABA has mapped out four fairly easy rides through rural and suburban areas. Since these trails are along roads traversed by cars and trucks, it is recommend that children under 14 ride with adults and that, before starting out, the rules of the road are reviewed as set forth in a pamphlet called "Bicycling on Virginia Roads: Laws and Safety Tips," available free from the State Bicycle Coordinator at 786-2964.

Three popular bicycle tours in the area are listed below:

- **Battlefield Park** Begins and ends at Fort Harrison, off Route 5, in eastern Henrico County. Tour the Civil War fort, marina and farmland.
- **Bellona Arsenal** Ride through suburban and rural Chesterfield County, beginning at Huguenot and Buford Road. Civil War arsenal site marked by cannon and gun mold. There are steep hills on this one.
- **Windsor Farms Tour** Begins at Locke Lane and ends at Cary Street. A half-mile ride through residential Richmond passing the Virginia House and Agecroft Hall.

Popular trails in other parts of the state:

- **Mount Vernon Bikeway** A 15-mile rural route past George Washington's home and along the Potomac River. For map, call (703) 285-2600.
- **Colonial Parkway** 22 miles linking Yorktown, Williamsburg and Jamestown Island. Ask for free Historic Triangle Bike Map when

you call 786-2964.

Area bicycle clubs sponsor tours all year long:

> Capital Community Cyclists, PO Box 29905, Richmond, 23229
> Richmond Area Bicycle Assn. (RABA), 266-BIKE

Maps of area and regional tours are available for purchase at Two Wheel Travel, 2934 Cary Street, 359-2453.

Bowling

The Richmond-Petersburg area has more than 330 bowling lanes, and at Plaza Bowl, children can bowl duckpins. The ball used in duckpins weighs about one half as much as a regular bowling ball, making it much easier to handle. There are leagues for children at most alleys. Many, like Plaza Bowl, have a special room and rates for birthday parties. Call for hours and fees, as they vary. The newest lanes are at the AMF Hanover Lanes, the state's largest and the most modern bowling center in the country.

North

> AMF Hanover Lanes, 56 lanes, 7313 Bell Creek Road,
>   Mechanicsville 559-2600

South

> Bowl America, 52 lanes, 7929 Midlothian Turnpike 320-7115
> Holiday Bowl, 24 lanes, 11400 Jefferson Davis Highway. 748-5635
> Kingpin Lanes, 32 lanes, 200 North Otterdale Road 378-7838
> Ten Pin Coliseum, 40 lanes, 325 Belt Boulevard 233-9801
> Plaza Bowl, 24 lanes, East Southside Plaza 233-8799

Southwest

Bowl America, 40 lanes, 11532 Hull Street Road 744-1500

East

Bowl America, 36 lanes, 5018 Williamsburg Road 222-5183

West

AMF Major League Bowl, 50 lanes, 8037 Shrader Road 747-9620
AMF Sunset Bowl, 32 lanes, 6450 W. Broad Street 282-0537

Boating, Tubing

Boat Rentals in State Parks See the chapter on State Parks for information on the following: Rowboats and paddleboats at Twin Lakes, paddleboats at Bear Creek, and sailboats at Holliday Lake.

Pedal boats can be rented on Fountain Lake in Byrd Park Memorial Day-Labor Day 11am-sundown every day. Park office: 780-6270.

Rent a canoe, rowboat or pedal boat and explore Beaver Lake at Pocahontas State Park. The lake connects with Swift Creek for exploring by canoe or rowboat. Weekend rentals begin when the weather warms up around April. Daily rentals Memorial Day-Labor Day, weekends only through about October. Pedal boats are priced at half-hour and hourly rates while canoes and rowboats are priced per hour or per day. Weekdays 10am-7pm, weekends 8am-7pm. Park office: 796-4255.

Tubing on the James There is a good 3-hour float from the Pony Pasture parking area to the James River Parks Visitor Center when the water level is between four and five feet. The trip can be really slow (about five hours) when the water is below three feet; then it might be more fun with flippers on. Only swimmers should tube, and younger than eight should wear life jackets with a crotch strap.

The Huguenot Bridge area is not recommended for tubing. The water is too slow here, the river parallels the roadway and it is not very scenic. Also, there is a real danger of getting too close to the Williams Dam—you may not see it until it is too late to get out. Even at lower water levels, it is never safe to run it and people have died here.

Canoeing

White water canoeing requires special skills, and a good way to learn these is to join an outdoors organization such as the following, which sponsor lessons and trips requiring varying degrees of skills:

Old Dominion Sierra Club, PO Box 803, Richmond, 23207.
Float Fishermen of Virginia, 2925 Westgate Drive, Richmond, 23235 (320-3240).

Chesterfield County Parks and Recreation Division also sponsors canoe trips and basic lessons for children and adults. See Parks and Recreation Departments, Chesterfield County.

Canoeing on the James River There are two good runs on the James within the city limits between the Huguenot Bridge and the James River Visitors Center, divided by the dangerous Williams Dam.

For flat-water canoeing, put in and take out at the Huguenot Woods landing below the Huguenot Bridge. The water is slow-moving enough at levels of five feet and under to paddle up- and downstream, exploring islands and sandbars. Stay well away from the Williams Dam, which is probably the most dangerous place on the river. It is located below the intersection of Rockfalls Drive and Riverside Drive and above the Pony Pasture parking area. Even when water level is low it is easy to misjudge the safety and try to run the dam. At this writing, more than 14 people have lost their lives when they were caught by the hydraulic force of water at the base of the dam.

Good white water canoeing can be found from the Pony Pasture parking area to the Visitors Center. Because the really big rapids at Belle Isle are just below the center, there is no safe boating beyond that point.

Of course, only experienced canoeists with life jackets should be on the river. For daily report of water level, call (800) 697-3373 for a menu of area climate reports and river readings.

The James River Basin Canoe Livery, Ltd. provides canoeing services to Richmond area children through scout and church groups. Call (540) 261-7334.

State Park and Preserve Canoeing See the chapter on State Parks and Preserves for information on canoe rentals at Chickahominy Wildlife Management Area and Harrison Lake National Fish Hatchery, as well as these state parks: Bear Creek Lake, Holliday Lake, Pocahontas and York River.

Camping

State parks offer a variety of camping amenities and environments for all levels of camping enthusiasts. The parks easiest to reach from Richmond are Bear Creek Lake State Park in Cumberland County and Pocahontas State Park in Chesterfield County.

For free information on public campgrounds in Virginia, call the Virginia Tourism Department for new guides and maps at (800) 922-6782. For reservations in Virginia call (800) 933-PARK outside Richmond or 225-3867 in Richmond. A camping directory is also available from the Virginia Campground Association of the Virginia Hospitality and Travel Association, 288-3065.

Fishing

Anyone between the ages of 16 and 65 is required to have a freshwater fishing license to fish in Virginia waters. Purchase one at a sporting goods store or from circuit court clerks (free list of these agents from the Commission of Game and Inland Fisheries, 367-1000). A special five-day permit can be purchased as well. No license is required for saltwater fishing or crabbing.

Fishing is allowed in the following parks:

Chesterfield County:

> Bryan, Byrd (Swain and Shields Lake), Forest Hill, James River Parks.
> Crump, Deep Run, Echo Lake, University of Richmond's Westhampton Lake, Deep Bottom Boat Landing.
> Rockwood, Point of Rocks, Swift Creek, Henricus, Pocahontas State Park, Dutch Gap Boat Landing, Appomattox River Boat Launch (see Canoeing).

Henrico County:

> Cheswick Park, Forest Avenue between Three Chopt and Skipwith Roads.
> Crump Park, 3400 Mountain Road 672-5106.
> Deep Bottom Park, 9525 Deep Bottom Road.
> Dorey Park, 2999 Darbytown Road.
> Echo Lake Park, 5701 Springfield Road.
> Osborne Boat Landing, 9680 Osborne Turnpike.
> Three Lakes Park, 400 Sausiluta Drive.

See also Harrison Lake National Fish Hatchery and Lake, Chickahominy Wildlife Management Area, Powhatan WMA, and State Parks.

For guides suggesting the best times and places in Virginia waters to catch fish, call the Virginia Game and Inland Fisheries at 367-1000. Also ask for their complete list of public boat ramps in the state.

For up-to-date information and lively articles, read the fishing column in the sports section of the *Richmond Times-Dispatch* with information on where fish are biting.

Boat Landings nearby:

Deep Bottom Boat Landing, boat ramp and pier fishing in eastern Henrico on the James. East Route 5, right on Kingsland Road, left on Deep Bottom Road 1.5 miles

Dutch Gap Boat Landing, ramp for launching trailered boats and a long, wooden fishing pier on the James in Chesterfield County. South I-95, East Coxendale Road to its end.

Appomattox River Boat Launch, see Canoeing.

Golf Courses

North

Belmont Park, par 71, 1600 Hilliard Road 266-4929. Site of the 1949 PGA Championship won by Sam Sneed.

The Crossings, par 72, 800 Virginia Center Parkway, Glen Allen 266-2254, 261-0000. Considered to be one of the best public courses in the state.

South

Bermuda, 9 holes, 14101 Ramblewood Drive, Chester 530-3800.

Birkdale, par 71, 8511 Royal Birkdale Drive, Chesterfield 739-8800.

The Highlands Golfers' Club, par 72, Highland Glen Drive, Chesterfield 796-4800. Opened in 1995.

River's Bend Country Club, par 71, 11700 Hogan's Alley Drive, Chester 530-1000. Home of touring professional Bobby Wadkins.

East

Brookwoods Golf Club, par 72, 7325 Club Drive, Quinton, New Kent County 932-3737.

Glenwood Golf Club, par 71, 3100 Creighton Road 226-1793.

Highland Springs Golf Club, par 70, 300 Lee Avenue, 737-4716.

Far East

Stonehouse Golf Club, 9550 Old Stage Road, Toano, VA 23168, (757) 566-1138. Opened in June 1996. Showcases the rugged beauty of eastern Virginia.

Royal New Kent, 5300 Bailey Road (State Route 155), Providence Forge 966-7023, (888) 253-4363. Opened in August 1996. Shades of Northern Ireland—not for the faint at heart.

West

The Hollows Golf Club, par 71, State Route 2, Box 1085, Montpelier 798-2949.

Mill Quarter Country Club, par 72, 1525 Mill Quarter Drive, Powhatan 598-4221.

Royal Virginia Golf Club, par 72, 3181 Duke Road, Hadensville 457-2041.

Sycamore Creek Golf Course, par 70, State Route 621, Goochland 784-3544.

Gymnastics

Hanover Olympiad 10094 Leadbetter Place, Ashland 550-3319. A large gymnastics center for ages 2 to 18 years. Preschool classes up to serious gymnastic training. Some summer and after school programs.

Richmond Olympiad A nationally recognized center for gymnastics and fitness programs for children ages 18 months to 18 years. Classes from "tumbling tots" to serious athletic training. Progressive classes allow children to develop according to individual ability in a non-competitive environment. Three locations:

10701 Trade Road, 794-2813
7431 White Pine Road, 275-7986
5000 Cox Road, 346-9089.

See also Recreation Centers in Appendix.

Hiking

Walkers, joggers and hikers in the Richmond metropolitan area have more than 200 miles of trails set aside for their own use, though some paths are used by bicyclists and horseback riders as well. The James River Park trails offer a wide variety of terrain to tackle, while city and county parks offer numerous guided trails in wooded areas and around lakes and ponds. For information on specific trails that are maintained by the state within an hour's drive of the city, hikers can call 786-5046 for the Virginia Division of State Parks or 367-1000 for the Virginia Department of Game and Inland Fisheries.

Here is a short listing of some of the newer trails managed locally.

Metro Richmond Greenways (Virginia Trails) This volunteer group promotes trails throughout the metro area and recently opened the mile-long Richmond-Ashland Trolley Line on the old roadbed of the former trolley line, which was halted in 1938. It extends from Gwathmey Church Road to Ashcake Road on the south side of Ashland on the right of way of the car line for a mile south of Ashland. For information about this worthwhile group and their activities to promote preservation and development of trails, call 798-4160.

Richmond The current project in development for the city features a trail of about a mile from the Interstate 95 overpass at Maury Street in South Richmond to Anarrow's Boat Marina downstream. This historic trail would begin a few feet from the eastern end of the new floodwall trail recently opened and go by the remains of the old Richmond slave docks and near the site of the original trading post around which Richmond grew. Richmond City Department of Recreation and Parks 780-5733.

Current trails include the following:

- **Byrd Park** South end of the Boulevard; 2 trails, 1.3 miles. Open parkland, lakes.
- **Forest Hill Park** Forest Hill Avenue and 34th Street; 2 trails, 1.5 miles. Lake, stream, open parkland, woodlands.
- **Huguenot Woods Trail** On Riverside Drive at the south end of Huguenot Bridge; 1 trail, 1.5 miles. Woodlands along river.
- **James River Flood Wall** South end of Manchester Bridge; 1.25 miles. Along the river.
- **James River Park** On Riverside Drive west of the Lee Bridge; 5 trails, 5.3 miles. Woodlands, fields along river.
- **Joseph Bryan Park** Hermitage Road and Westbrook Avenue; 1 trail, 1 mile. Parkland around lake.
- **Maymont** Pumphouse Road at north end of Westover Hills Bridge; 4 trails, 4 miles. Parkland and gardens.
- **Pine Camp** Azalea Avenue and Old Brook Road; 2 trails, 1.8 miles. Fields and woodlands.
- **Pony Pasture Park** Riverside Drive and Club Drive; 4 trails, 1.5 miles. Fields and woodlands.
- **Powhite Park** Chippenham Parkway and Jahnke Road; 3 trails, 1.5 miles. Fields, woodlands, stream.
- **Riverside Park** Tredegar Street under the Lee Bridge; 2 trails, 2.5 miles. Park trails along river, on Belle Isle.

Hanover County The Hanover County Department of Parks and Recreation (537-6165) opened a half-mile trail near the Cold Harbor Battlefield Park. The trail starts at the Watt House parking lot and goes through woods and along a creek. The trail complements several miles of trails in the Cold Harbor park, which is maintained by the National Park Service.

Current trails include the following:

Hanover Poor Farm Park State Route 54, 3.5 miles west of Ashland, behind Liberty Middle School; 3 trails, 7 miles. Fields, woodlands.

Richmond-Ashland Trolley Line Trail in Ashland. Gwaltney Church Road to Ashcake Road; 1 mile. Woodlands.

North Anna Battlefield Park State Route 684, 10 miles north of Ashland; 1 trail, 2.4 miles. Reservation required. Fields, woodlands, river.

Richmond Battlefield Parks Cold Harbor Trail, State Route 156 east of Mechanicsville; 1.1 miles. Fields, woodlands.

Henrico County A new quarter-mile trail at Fort Harrison near Varina in eastern Henrico County allows visitors to see previously inaccessible parts of the fort. Henrico County Division of Recreation and Parks 672-5100.

Current trails include the following:

Cheswick Park 1700 Forest Avenue; 1 trail, 1 mile. Fields, woodlands.

Crump Park 3400 Mountain Road; 2 trails, 1.2 miles. Fields and woodlands.

Deep Run Park 9900 Ridgefield Parkway; 4 trails, 2.8 miles. Fields, woodlands, lake.

Dorey Park 2999 Darbytown Road; 3 trails, 2 miles. Fields, woodlands, lake.

Dunncroft Castle Point Park 4900 Francistown Road; 1 trail, 0.52 mile. Fields, woodlands.

Echo Lake Park 5701 Springfield Road; 1 trail, 0.6 mile. Fields, woodlands, lake.

Hidden Creek Park 2415 Brockway Lane; 1 trail, 0.4 mile. Fields, woodlands.

Springfield Park 4600 Springfield Road; 0.4 mile walking trail. Fields, woodlands.

Three Lakes Park 400 Sausiluta Drive; 3 trails, 1.5 miles. Fields, woodlands, lakes.

Vawter Street Park 4501 Vawter Avenue; 2 trails, 2.4 miles. Fields, woodlands, swamp trails.

Richmond Battlefield Park Battlefield Park Road south of State Route 5 at Varina; 3 trails, 2.3 miles. Fields, woodlands, Civil War fortifications.

Chesterfield County Parks and Recreation Department (748-1623) has several trail projects in the planning stages, including a new self-guided trail at Clover Hill Athletic Complex near Clover Hill High School. The county is also developing its new 60-acre Robious Landing Park and was recently awarded a federal grant to develop the 46-acre Falling Creek Linear Park.

Current trails include the following:

Henricus Historical Park Coxendale Road at Dutch Gap boat landing; 1 trail, 1.3 miles. Trail through woodlands along river.

Huguenot Park Robious Road and Woodmont Drive; 1 trail, 1 mile. Fields, woodlands.

Iron Bridge Park State Route 10 and Airport Road; 3 trails, 5 miles. Fields, woodlands.

Pocahontas State Park State Route 655 west of Chesterfield Court House; 7 trails, 12.4 miles. Fields, woodlands, lakes, streams.

Point of Rocks Park State Route 746, 2 miles west of State Route 10 in Bermuda Hundred; 3 trails, 1.5 miles. Fields, woodlands, marshlands along river.

Rockwood Park U.S. 360 and Courthouse Road; 5 trails, 3.4 miles. Fields, woodlands, stream.

Horseback Riding

The Richmond area features more than 250 miles of public trails for horses and their riders. In addition to the numerous public trails, there are nearly two dozen riding academies and stables for persons interested in equestrian sports. Information about horseback trails in the Richmond area and around Virginia can be obtained from the Virginia Commission of Game and Inland Fisheries (367-1000) and the Virginia Division of State Parks (786-1712).

Pocahontas State Park and Forest 796-4255. You can ride your own horse on the bridle paths in the park and the state forest adjacent to it. For information and maps call the Park Supervisor. There are no rental horses available at Pocahontas.

Allegheny Stables and Equestrian Center Powhatan 379-2970.

Amherst Farms Hanover 779-2608. Boarding, lessons and training.

Autumn Wood Farm I-295 and Nuckols Road, 14190 Nash Lane, Glen Allen 798-6424. Features an indoor and outdoor lighted area.

Cedar Knoll Farm Glen Allen 749-3725. Boarding, shows and birthdays featured here.

Chickahominy Lakeside Riding 13501 Pocahontas Trail, Lanexa 966-5852. Rentals, lessons and ponies for parties.

Clarke's Barn Route 620, 749-4344. Boarding and training, seven days a week.

Deep Run Hunt Pony Club & Genito Pony Club Manakin-Sabot District Commissioner 741-3879. Meetings, clinics, trail rides, mock hunts, summer camp for up to age 21 where children learn to train, groom and show horses. Horse ownership not prerequisite for membership. Annual fee includes newsletter and clinics.

Foxmeade Farm 12150 Robious Road, Midlothian 794-5820. Private and group lessons age 4-adult. Summer day camp; schooling shows spring, summer and fall; and transportation to out-of-town shows. Lighted outdoor arena for evening classes.

Innisfree Farm Manakin-Sabot 784-5139. Year-round classes for age 7-adult; schooling shows and day camp in summer; mock hunts and trail rides; transportation to shows; and instructors take videos of shows to record progress. Fox hunt prep clinics for over age 12. Lighted arena for evening instruction. Private lessons.

Level Green Riding School Powhatan 794-8463. Private or small group (5) classes from age 6. Elementary dressage taught, with emphasis on hunting and jumping. Trail riding; four clinics per year; shows in conjunction with 4-H; nine-week summer camp. Staff will break, train, board horses and will transport students to shows and coach them.

Walnut Knoll Manakin-Sabot 784-4189. Lessons for boarders only. Ages 6 and up learn to groom and take up their mounts in private or small groups (4). Schooling shows and riding trails available to students. Transportation to and coaching at away shows.

Ice-Skating & Sledding

Occasionally Richmond will have several consecutive days of weather cold enough for outdoor ice-skating, and there are usually several good snows for sledding. Skating is allowed on Fountain Lake in Byrd Park. During heavy freezes the ice is checked for thickness, and public announcements are made when it is safe for skating.

Sledding is allowed in any of the parks when there is enough snow. The best hills are in the Richmond city parks. Sledding on sheets of metal is prohibited, as is the use of motorized devices. Parents should accompany children, especially in the evenings, as in the past people have been injured on crowded hills.

Ice-Skating, Indoors

Southampton Recreation Association in Stratford Hills has an enclosed rink for residents of the area. Membership is required. Open

December-March, lessons for age 6-adult. Call 272-7401 between 9am and 1pm.

SkateNation Johnston Willis Drive, 378-7465. Formerly known as the Ice Forum, the regulation NHL-sized rink is open seven days a week, 7am to midnight. Call for weekday and weekend prices. Skate rental is available.

SkateNation West 4350 Pouncey Tract Road, Glen Allen 364-0151. Brand new West End location features two NHL-sized rinks. Open seven days a week. Skate rental available. Call for prices and programs.

Marathons

Richmond Times-Dispatch Marathon 649-6738. Although there are a variety of races and walks throughout the Richmond area, the longest-running marathon is the October event sponsored by the Richmond Times-Dispatch. In addition to the 26.2-mile race, a half-marathon and a 5-mile race are offered to more than 2,500 entrants of all ages and sizes.

For the **Richmond Roadrunners Club** race and information hotline, call 360-2672.

Roller-Skating

North of the James River

Golden Skate World 3214 Skipwith Road 270-2314. Skating and hockey lessons are offered here at various times throughout the week. Open evenings Wednesday-Thursday 7:30-10pm. Friday until midnight. Saturday 10am-noon is for 12 and under accompanied by a parent. Open skate Saturday 2pm-4:30pm and 8pm-11pm. Sunday is family day, 3pm-

5pm. Call for admission prices and skate rental info. Occasionally open in the daytime for Henrico County school holidays.

Skate America 6521 Mechanicsville Turnpike 730-3252. Parties often scheduled Monday and Wednesday, so call for weekly schedule. Birthday parties scheduled during open skate on Tuesday, Saturday and Sunday. Open Hanover County school holidays and teachers' work days.

Skateland 516 North Washington Highway, Ashland 798-6550. Skating and speed skating lessons are offered. Family skate times Tuesday evenings and Sunday afternoon. Wednesday afternoons, 3:30-5:30pm, ages 10 and under. Open Henrico and Hanover County school holidays and snow days. Evening hours are seasonal. Call for price info.

South of the James River

All American Skate 5500 Hull Street 233-7215. Call daily to find out evening schedule, as private parties and fund-raisers are often scheduled weeknights. Skating lessons are offered, and there are organized games and special skates. Open City and Chesterfield County school holidays and snow days with special skate rates, treats and drawings.

Skate-A-Way 3330 Speeks Drive 674-5070. Two maplewood skating floors—one is only for beginners. Full service snack bar. Pro-shop. Open Chesterfield County school holidays and teachers' work days (except Fridays). Call for skating times, admissions fees and skate rental information.

Skateland 2300 Southland Drive, Chester 748-0379. Call for prices and more information on skating times. Special summer hours run June-August.

Skateland 4902 Williamsburg Road 222-5765. Private parties Monday and Wednesday nights. Lessons Saturday morning 10am-noon ages 12 and under, with parent. Open skate Saturday 2-5pm and 7:30-midnight. Sunday 2:30-7pm and 8:30-11:30pm. Open Henrico school holidays and snow days.

Skiing

Family ski trips are sponsored by the Richmond Ski Club, which also holds social and informative meetings during winter months. Call 741-FUNN. Also, the Virginia Ski Club, 262-3275.

Virginia Ski Resorts

Bryce Resort, Basye (540) 856-2121, ski report (540) 856-2151.
Massanutton, Harrisonburg (800) 334-6086, ski report (540) 289-9441.
The Homestead, Hot Springs (800) 336-5771, report (540) 839-5500.
Wintergreen, Wintergreen 325-2200.
Cascade, Fancy Gap (540) 728-3161.

Local numbers to call for ski reports

Alpine Outfitters: 794-4172
Par 3 Ski Shop: 270-4264

Swimming

City of Richmond Free Swimming Swimming is free for all citizens at Richmond's 11 pools, with instruction for all skill levels. The city operates two indoor pools:

Calhoun Community Center pool, 436 Calhoun Street 780-4751, open year-round
Swansboro pool, 3160 Midlothian Turnpike 780-5088, open September-May.

The city's nine outdoor pools are open from mid-June to Labor Day. Lessons are offered throughout the week. Swim teams for ages 9-16

Sports

compete with teams from other communities. For more information on pools, lessons or teams, call the Aquatics Coordinator, Richard Tyre, at 780-5088.

Outdoor city pools (Note that some of the phone numbers will be out-of-service during the off-season).

Northside

Battery Park Pool, 2719 Dupont Circle 321-0749.
Hotchkiss Field Pool, 701 Brookland Park Boulevard 780-8610.

East end

Chimborazo, 2900 East Grace Street 780-4566.
Fairmount, 2000 "U" Street 780-4577.
Powhatan Community Center, 1000 Apperson Street 780-8583.
Woodville, 2000 North 28th Street 780-4563.

Southside

Bellemeade Community Center, 1800 Lynhaven Avenue 780-5035.
Blackwell-Maury Community Center, 238 East 14th Street 780-8832.

Westend

Randolph Community Center, 239 South Lombardy Street 780-6222.

St. Joseph's Villa Route 1 and Parham Road 266-2447. Pool and lessons. Open to general public as well as members for a reasonable fee. Classes for preschoolers and up. Call 1-4pm on Tuesdays and Thursdays.

Jewish Community Center 5403 Monument Avenue 288-6091. Open swim lessons for members only, but you don't have to be Jewish to join. Parent-tot classes for ages 12 months-36 months. Lessons for all ages meeting once a week for eight weeks in winter, and every day for two weeks in summertime. There is also a swim team.

Red Cross 409 East Main Street 780-2250. Children and adults have learned to swim with the help of The American Red Cross, Greater Richmond Chapter. Taught at pools all over the area, their tried-and-tested program includes basic and advanced swimming skills for children.

YMCA Since 1854, Richmond's YMCAs offer swim lessons for adults, children and families:

- Chester, 3011 West Hundred Road 748-9622
- Chickahominy, 5401 Whiteside Road, Sandston 737-9622
- Downtown, 2 West Franklin Street 644-9622
- Manchester, 7540 Hull Street Road 276-9622
- North Richmond, 4207 Old Brook Road, near Ginter Park 329-9622
- Patrick Henry, 405 England Street, Ashland 798-0057
- Shady Grove, 4024-C Cox Road, Glen Allen 346-1800
- Tuckahoe, 9211 Patterson Avenue 740-9622.

YWCA 6 North Fifth Street 643-6761. The Health and Wellness Center offers swimming lessons for children.

In the surrounding counties, more than 90 recreation centers and associations offer swimming and competitive swim teams. Many are associated with new and old developments.

Pocahontas State Park 10301 State Park Road in Chesterfield County 768-4350. Large, modern outdoor pool with several diving boards, two slides and a wading pool. Open daily, 10am-7pm, Memorial Day-Labor Day. To avoid crowds on holidays and weekends, come during the week, 10am-2pm, and Sunday mornings. Under 3 free.

Team Sports

The county Departments of Parks and Recreation for Chesterfield, Henrico, Hanover and Richmond offer many youth leagues for girls and boys. Leagues are generally seasonal; and offerings include baseball, basketball, football, gymnastics, soccer, softball and wrestling.

Contact your Parks and Recreation Department for further information:

Chesterfield: 748-1623
Hanover: 798-8062, 730-6165, 537-6165, 227-3377
Henrico: 672-5100
Richmond: 780-5733

The following is information on baseball, softball, and soccer summer leagues, which are very popular during summer break:

Little League Baseball and Softball for boys and girls

Chesterfield County Little Leagues Twenty-six independent leagues, open to boys and girls, practice at the following elementary schools: Bellwood, Bensley Beulah, Chaulkely, Clover Hill, Davis, Enon, Ettrick Falling Creek, Gates, Gordon, Harrowgate, Hening, Hopkins, Matoaca, Midlothian, Reams, Robious, Salem Church and Swift Creek. For more information contact the county's Department of Parks and Recreation at 748-1623. Co-ed soft- and fast-pitch softball is organized under the Chesterfield Youth Softball Association (call Mildred Burrell, 275-6997) and the Chesterfield United Girls Softball League (call Milton Simmons, 743-1336).

Henrico County Little Leagues Ten baseball leagues for boys and girls are organized in these geographical areas: Bethlehem, Tuckahoe, Glen Lea, Glen Allen, Sandston, Montrose, Lakeside, Highland Springs, Chamberlayne and Varina. In addition, Henrico County is home to the Western Girls and the Bethlehem Girls, both slow-pitch softball leagues.

For more information on practice schedules and team contacts, call Andy Crane, Department of Parks and Recreation at 672-5156.

Hanover County Little Leagues

Ashland Little League, Pete Taylor, 798-4128 or Wayne Melton, 752-4955.
Beaverdam Youth Association, Debbie Murphy, 227-3664.
Atlee Little League, 730-0327.
Atlee Youth Sports, Danny Longest, 730-7565.
Mechanicsville Youth Association, Sherell Cole, 746-0598.
Rockville Little League, Wayne Kent, 883-6915 or Gene Smith, 883-6509.
Western Regional Youth Association, Wayne Kent, 883-6915.

Hanover also sponsors **Challenger baseball** for children aged 6-12 who have disabilities. Children from all counties in the Richmond and surrounding area are welcome to participate. Call Lisa Marshall or Kathy Healey at 746-0082 for more information.

Richmond Little Leagues Presidents of leagues change frequently. For the most current information on whom to contact, call Richard Smith, Sports Supervisor, at the City of Richmond Parks and Recreation Department, 780-8117 or 782-4267. Several independent leagues are divided among the following areas in Richmond:

East Richmond Little League, John L. Taylor, 225-7280 or 649-7688.
North Richmond Little League, Rebecca Beard, 262-3069 or 780-8144.
South Richmond Little League, Michael Doyle, 745-2048.
West Richmond Little League, Jack Molenkamp, 285-7734 or 788-8655.

Police Athletic League 14th and Maury Streets 780-5856. Offers programs for children 12 and under and 13-16.

Salvation Army Boys and Girls Club 3701 R Street 222-3122. Children 12 and under.

Virginia Randolph Community Center 780-6227. Offers T-ball and a program for children 12 and under.

Westhampton Community Center 5800 Patterson Avenue 285-1416. T-ball.

Soccer

Soccer programs throughout the metropolitan area allow children as young as 5 years old to learn how to play this fun sport. Development of skills is emphasized in the younger programs, while more competitive games can be found in the older levels of the leagues with "traveling" teams. Teams are open to both boys and girls, and clubs are formed according to geographic area, although players are not required to play for the club nearest their home.

City of Richmond Leagues Parks and Recreation Department sponsors teams that play in playgrounds all over town, with a fall and spring season. For a list of teams and their practice areas call 780-6175.

    F.C. Richmond, 897-2997.
    Richmond Neighborhood Soccer Association, 275-1636.

Chesterfield County Soccer Leagues

    Chesterfield Soccer Club, 796-3030.
    Midlothian Youth Soccer League, 744-8505.
    Pocoshock Valley Youth League, 276-1454.

Powhatan Soccer Association, 598-2533.
Reams Soccer Club, Pete Neal or Mark Groth, 794-2584.

Hanover County

Atlee Youth Soccer/Arsenal FC, Craig Taylor, 746-8636.
Ashland Youth Soccer League, Jack Dyer, 227-3757.
Western Regional Youth Association, Elenor Lewis, 883-6387.

Henrico County Leagues

Eastern Football Club United, 737-9622
Richmond Strikers Soccer Club, 288-GOAL.
Richmond Capitals Soccer Club, 261-KICK.

Tennis

City of Richmond tennis courts are free to use and available on a first-come-first-"served" basis for an hour of play when instruction or tournaments are not in session. City Parks and Recreation offers free instruction for youth during the summer. For more information on courts near you, call the city tennis specialist, 780-4179.

Henrico County Parks and Recreation offers tennis for ages 6-18 at

Belmont Park Recreation Center, 1600 Hilliard Road,
Godwin High School, 2101 Pump Road, and
Varina High School, 7900 Messer Road.

Call 649-0566 for a schedule and fees.

Chesterfield County has courts located at most parks and athletic complexes (See Parks).

Chapter 6

Performing Arts and Festivities

Theater
Film
Music
Dance
Arts Instruction
Outdoor Performances and Free Concerts
Seasonal Events

Norris Guncheon, Age 4½
"Looking at Christmas lights at the James Center"

Theater

Theatre IV, the touring Richmond Theatre Company for Children, and the various summertime productions offered by community theater groups and Recreation Department volunteers specialize in productions for youngsters, delighting them with fables, fairy tales and history, as well as presenting safety and other issues. The community theaters we include present at least one family-oriented play each season. There are several plays presented at Dogwood Dell Festival of the Arts, and organizations that teach theater skills to children present plays to the public as the culmination of their season's efforts.

Older families have a much broader list of theaters from which to choose—professional productions at the Carpenter Center and the recently reopened Richmond's Landmark Theater (formerly the Mosque), community theater plays, college productions and dinner theater. For listings and reviews, see Style Weekly (Tuesday), or Richmond Newspapers (Thursday, Saturday and Sunday). [See Publications.] In all cases, please call to verify productions, show times and pricing.

Applause Unlimited 264-0299. This unique company utilizes puppets and live performers in their productions, which tour the Henrico school system as well as public arenas for all to enjoy. Classic theater and original adaptations are their forte.

Barksdale Theatre at Willow Lawn 282-2620. The Barksdale is the oldest theater company in the metropolitan area. Musicals, comedies, and dramas fill the bill each season with special Saturday morning shows for kids.

Chamberlayne Actors Theater through the North Chamberlayne Civic Association 262-9760. This all-volunteer group presents three family-oriented shows each season at the Chamberlayne Civic Association building, 319 North Wilkinson Road near Chamberlayne Road.

Chesterfield Theatre Company (formerly John Rolfe Players) 748-0698. The area's oldest community theater performs in Chesterfield County schools. Three shows are presented during the

Performing Arts and Festivities

school year and are sponsored partly by the Chesterfield Department of Parks and Recreation.

HATTheatre 343-6364. This company teaches theater to children in grades 1-12 and produces one show each season, with casting open to adults and children throughout the community. Performances are held at 1124A Westbriar Drive.

Henrico Teen Theater Company 672-5115. The Henrico County Department of Recreation and Parks sponsors a group of young actors in a summer production at the John Rolfe Middle School.

Henrico Theater Company 672-5115. Adult community theater group sponsored by Henrico Division of Parks and Recreation. Each season, volunteers present four performances at the Belmont Park Recreation Center at 1600 Hilliard Road. Of special interest to children is the family-oriented Christmas show and visit from Santa Claus.

Lee Playhouse in Fort Lee 734-6630. KidKapers is the name of the children's division of productions by this long-running community theater.

Mystery Dinner Playhouse 8099 West Broad Street 649-2583. Features interactive and entertaining productions of the "Mystery for Kids." 3-4 productions per year, with performances every Saturday.

Richmond Department of Recreation and Parks 780-7000. As part of the Festival of the Arts in the Dogwood Dell outdoor ampitheater at Byrd Park, this county organization utilizes volunteers for its three summer productions.

Richmond Neighborhood Players 342-0960. This community group offers three productions per season at the Modlin Center for Performing Arts at the University of Richmond.

Richmond Theatre Company for Children 644-3444, (888) 689-1962. This touring company performs free shows at area malls, day-care centers and libraries, as well as out of state along the East Coast. They can also be booked for school performances. A participatory theater focusing on ages 3-8 and using educational, non-violent, morality themes. Shows last for about 45 minutes and stress audience participation. The group performs ten different shows per season, year-round. See newspapers for schedule.

School of the Performing Arts in the Richmond Community (SPARC) 355-2662. Since 1981, this school has taught acting, voice and dance to students (ages 5-18) who have gone on to perform in theater groups and productions. Each summer, a huge cast is involved in a vibrant musical in the Empire Theatre on West Broad Street.

Swift Creek Mill Playhouse U.S. Route 1 in Colonial Heights 748-5203. Set in a 350-year-old grist mill, the Swift Creek Mill Playhouse features a series of daytime productions for children to complement their evening dinner theater presentations.

Theatre IV Empire Theatre 114 West Broad Street 344-8050. The Family Playhouse series specializes in entertaining the whole family. This nationally known, professional, award-winning group performs at the historic Empire Theatre, a restored 1911 Victorian building, the oldest theater in the state. Themes include fairy tales, fables, history, safety and family issues.

A variety of subscriptions are available for five annual shows with individual show tickets at the door. Performances are Wednesday, Thursday and Friday at 10:15am, Friday at 7pm, Saturday at 10am, 2pm and 7pm, and Sunday at 2:30pm. Ample parking and lots at Grace and Foushee Streets or Franklin and Jefferson Streets.

Theatre VCU 10 North Brunswick Street 828-1514. Located in the Fan, this theater produces four main stage student and faculty productions at the Raymond Hodges Theatre at the Performing Arts Center.

Theatre Virginia 353-6161. Formerly the Virginia Museum Theatre, presents their shows at the Virginia Museum of Fine Arts at 2800 Grove Avenue but also performs educational outreach programs throughout the area.

Performing Arts and Festivities

Theatre with Children for Children 828-2772. The Community School of the Performing Arts at VCU sponsors this company, which features students from the school ages 6-17 in touring companies as well as a December musical and a series of spring productions at the VCU Music Center.

Virginia Historical Theatre at Berkeley Plantation 323-6477. Formed to produce historical dramas, this theater presents its shows at the Berkeley Hundred Ampitheatre at the Berkeley Plantation on the James River.

Film

Byrd Theatre 2908 West Cary Street 353-9911. Built in 1928, the Byrd is an elegant theater with marble walls, gilded ceilings, scalloped curtains and a beautiful Czechoslovakian chandelier hanging in the lobby. Second-run and classic movies are shown for an admission of 99¢. No one under age three admitted.

Regal NEI Ridge Cinemas 1510 East Ridge Road 285-1567. Seven screens fill the bill here with special weekday morning showings for children during the summer.

Regal Virginia Center Commons 14 10091 J.E.B. Stuart Highway in Glen Allen (at Virginia Center Commons) 261-5411. Not to be outdone by any other area theater, this Regal cinema offers you a choice of 14 different films at any one time, with special weekday morning showings for children during the summer.

Plaza Drive-In Theatre 4730 North Southside Plaza 232-0022. Though it shows second-run films during its season, the Plaza Drive-In is remarkable for what it is—a single-screen outdoor movie theater operating during a time when multiplexes and indoor cinemas are the rage. Promising family entertainment, the Plaza is a fun experience for the whole family, especially with the occasional special programming nights featuring "B" movies.

Music

Besides the major musical and dance series listed here, there are many concerts presented by churches, schools and colleges, performing arts organizations, community choruses, concert bands and orchestras. Many of these groups present a free, annual performance at Dogwood Dell Festival of the Arts in the summertime (see Outdoor Concerts).

Classical and traditional music is everywhere in the Richmond area in a variety of venues. Though most are promoted to adults, children's concerts are an occasional highlight.

Carpenter Center Box office: 225-9000. Presents a variety of music, theater and dance by nationally known artists.

Musical Mondays at Maymont 358-7166. Maymont continues with their series of free brass band concerts during the summer on the carriage house lawn.

Richmond Classical Players 288-6056. This string orchestra features music from the baroque to contemporary.

Richmond Philharmonic 673-4001. Volunteer civic orchestra offering several concerts each season.

Richmond Symphony Box office: 788-1212. Presenting several series each season including classical, jazz, popular, Broadway and movie music at the Carpenter Center, Richmond's Landmark Theater (formerly the Mosque) and the VCU Performing Arts Center. Performances on Friday, Saturday, Sunday and Monday evenings, with student discounts for season tickets.

Virginia Opera 643-6004. Several productions each season are presented in Richmond at the Carpenter Center.

Virginia Museum of Fine Arts 367-0844. A summer series of pop music called "Jumpin' in July."

Performing Arts and Festivities

If you like to make music, there are quite a few community bands and organizations that are looking for students:

All Saints Choir of Men and Boys 288-7811

Henrico Community Band, contact Cheryl Miltonberger 225-4107

Richmond Symphony Young Performers' Program, for beginning string students 788-4717

For popular music fans, there are quite a few venues and organizations sponsoring rock, blues, jazz, country and more throughout the year:

Classic Amphitheatre at Strawberry Hill 600 East Laburnum 228-3213. This outdoor pavilion plays host to some of the biggest names in music today with concerts beginning in mid-April and running through October. Of special highlight are the shows booked during the run of the State Fair of Virginia in September. Tickets are sold at the Fairgrounds ticket office (228-3200) or by phone (262-8100).

Richmond's Landmark Theater (The Mosque) 6 North Laurel Street 780-8226. Seating more than 3,000 people, this recently renovated concert hall is unique to the area and features R&B, gospel, rock, pop and occasional children's shows.

The Richmond Coliseum Seventh and Leigh Streets 780-4970. More than just a sports venue, the Coliseum offers rock, rap and pop concerts as well. To hear who is playing next, call 780-4956.

Dance

Concert Ballet of Virginia 798-0945. This is a community ballet company that produces a fall, winter and spring program at the Women's Club Auditorium. Their holiday production of "The Nutcracker" will also tour area high schools.

Richmond Ballet 359-0906. This professional company, the 16th largest in the country, offers the classic holiday production of "The Nutcracker" in December, as well as regular productions each season at Theatre Virginia and the Carpenter Center for the Performing Arts.

Colonial Dance Club 744-3264. The members of this 20-year-old group enjoy English dances that started in the 1500s as well as Colonial America dances.

Elegba Folklore Society 644-3900. This performing ensemble also teaches dance and drumming classes at their Cultural Center at 114 East Franklin Street (see Chapter 2). They also offer workshops and performance/lectures around the Richmond area.

Arts Instruction

Theater Instruction

The following companies present children as cast and crew, teaching drama skills as well as presenting plays:

School of the Performing Arts in the Richmond Community (SPARC) 355-2662. Classes in theater arts for ages 7-18, including instruction in acting, dance, voice, improvisation and character development. Children learn to work together, taking part in script writing and helping to develop shows. Special classes are available for the hearing impaired.

Three sessions are offered per year, each followed by a premiere performance, admission free to public. The group also performs at community events, shopping malls and schools.

Fall and winter sessions begin in September and January, meeting once a week for 11 weeks. Summer session in June and July meets five days a week for six weeks. Interviews are held prior to acceptance of 9-18 year olds.

Performing Arts and Festivities

Theatre IV at Collegiate School 741-9714. Theatre IV offers two summer programs that give children in grades 5-8 and 9-12 the rare opportunity to work on an actual production at Collegiate's Oates Theater for the Arts. Auditions are held in late April.

Acting Out with RTC 644-3444. Offers theater education for children ages 5-18. Classes are offered at the Jewish Community Center and can be booked on site. This program is offered year-round in 6-, 8- and 10-week blocks.

VCU Community School for the Performing Arts 1015 Grove Avenue 828-2772. Drama classes to introduce children, ages 6-16, to all aspects of theater arts including mime, dramatic interpretation, movement, music and technical knowledge of theater and its disciplines. In addition to classes, children may take part in the touring company, SODA, taking shows to area schools and out of state, performing in theaters and on television and film. The elaborate Christmas production is open to the public, with the performance at the VCU Performing Arts Center on Park Avenue. Free parking.

For more information contact Una Harrison, the director.

Henrico Teen Theater A free summer program for K-7th graders, with auditions in early June, rehearsals three times a week through July and free public performances at Belmont Park at the end of July.

Plays usually deal with the problems faced by today's youth. Children are involved in all aspects of production, contributing ideas to the script, helping to make costumes and sets, suggesting ideas for lighting and sound.

Practices are at the old Hermitage Country Club building, 1600 Hilliard Road, where performances are staged in the old ballrooms. The group also travels to other locations upon request.

For more information about taking part in the program and for performance schedule, call cultural arts director Larkin Brown at 672-5115.

Music Instruction

If you'd like to learn to make music, the **Richmond Music Teachers Association** acts as a referral for teachers of flute, guitar, organ, piano, violin, voice and other instruments 744-3710.

Neighborhood School of the Arts 359-5049. After-school programs are offered for children in grades 2-5. Classes are held at Ginter Park Presbyterian, 3601 Seminary Avenue.

Swift Creek Academy of the Performing Arts 2808 Fox Chase Lane in Brandermill 744-2801. Children ages 4-18 are given private instruction in fall, spring and summer semesters of piano, guitar, keyboard, woodwinds, violin and percussion as well as chorus and music theory. Adult classes are also available.

VCU Community School of the Performing Arts Department of Music, 1015 Grove Avenue 828-2772. Classes and private instruction in standard orchestra and band instruments, voice, guitar, piano and keyboards; Suzuki-method violin, piano and flute; composition and theory. Open to all ages, beginning to advanced levels. Fall, spring and summer semesters with classes at VCU Music Center. Full and partial music scholarships awarded based on talent and financial need.

Suzuki method is designed for very young children and based on the assumption that children can learn music the same way they learn their native language: rough listening, imitation, repetition and rich motivational environment provided by parents. Parents attend lessons and assist with home practice. Piano and violin begin at age 3, flute at age 4. Classes can be scheduled weekdays between 9am and 9 pm and Saturdays 9am-3pm, at VCU, elementary schools or other arranged locations.

Virginia Union University Community Music Academy 257-5669. This academy offers private instruction in theory and composition, voice, piano and organ.

Dance Instruction

Park and Recreation Department Dance Lessons Among the variety of dance lessons offered by area park and recreation departments are ballet, tap, ballroom, clogging and Latin dance. Most departments offer two sessions, beginning in September and January, and fees are usually considerably less than commercial dance studios, sometimes free. Current offerings are listed in quarterly brochures available at library branches, or call your Parks and Recreation Department:

Chesterfield County: 748-1623
Hanover County: 537-6165
Henrico County: 672-5100
City of Richmond: 780-5733

Youth Ballet Program City of Richmond community centers, 780-6047. Free program open to all, ages 4 and up. Meeting September-May. Call early to reserve a space in this popular program, directed by Annette Holt. There is also a ballet program for the visually or hearing impaired.

Jewish Community Center of Richmond 288-6091. Classes in creative movement and dance are offered for ages 3 to adult.

Ann Catherine Cross School of Dance 6906 Cold Harbor Road 730-1740. Ballet, jazz, tap, hip-hop classes and more are offered to children.

Cat's Cap 6001 Grove Avenue 288-2804. This creative arts program runs in June and July at St. Catherine's School. Features dance among other arts programs.

Chesterfield School of Ballet 4500 West Hundred Road in Chester 748-6177. Introduction to dance, focus on coordination and rhythmic skills for ages 4-6. Class for children ages 4 and up.

Children's Creative Workshop 7027 Three Chopt Road 288-7735. For preschoolers: tumbling, creative movement and creative storytelling with music plus ballet, creative movement and modern dance. Ballet, tap and jazz for ages 2 and up.

Concert Ballet of Virginia 103 East Main Street 798-0945. Dance classes for children ages 3 and up are offered in ballet, pointe, modern, tap and jazz with summer classes leading to performances with the Concert Ballet at Dogwood Dell. Auditions are held each summer for the annual holiday production of "The Nutcracker."

Dance and Theatre Unlimited 2470 Anderson Highway 598-8159. Children ages 2½ and up are offered classes in ballet, tap, jazz and pointe.

Dance Masters 5008 Lakeside Avenue 262-9587. Traditional ballet, tap and jazz classes are offered to children ages 3 and up.

Encore Performing Arts Studio 10350 Iron Bridge Road, Chester 748-3642. Classes in ballet, tap, pointe, combination and jazz are offered.

Hale School of Dance 117 England Street, Ashland 798-3011. Creative movement, pre-ballet and tumbling for preschoolers; ballet and tap for ages 5 and older.

Jessica Morgan School of Dance 13989 Hull Street Road 739-7600. Ballet, jazz, tap, pointe and creative movement are offered to children ages 2 and up.

Martinique School of Dance
    8009 Buford Court 272-9152
    4368 Laburnum Avenue 222-3728.
Children ages 3 and up are offered classes in ballet, tap, jazz and pointe.

Monument Avenue Dance Studio 2600 Monument Avenue 353-7913. Beginning ballet softshoe and tap for children 3 and up. Classical ballet arts at age 7. Jazz for ages 9 and up.

Performing Arts and Festivities

Regency Dance Academy Quioccasin Station Shopping Center 740-4966. Tap, jazz, pointe, lyrical, ballet and hip-hop classes are offered.

Richmond Ballet 359-0906. Offers a summer session in jazz, modern and ballet as well as creative movement for children of all ages.

Richmond Ballet Center for Dance
614 Lombardy Street 359-0906 ext. 225
1201 Mall Drive near Chesterfield Towne Center 379-0525.
Creative movement, pre-ballet, ballet and jazz dance for ages 4 and up.

Richmond Dance Center 8906-E West Broad Street in Loehman's Plaza 747-0533. Ballet, tap, jazz and creative dance for ages 2 and up and at all levels. Parent/child classes are also available.

Robert School of Dance 8229 Hull Street Road 276-7239. Classes in ballet, tap, jazz and acrobatics are offered for children ages 2 and up.

Royal Dance Company 2021 Huguenot Village 272-2108. Creative movement and pre-ballet for 3-4 year olds; ballet and tap for ages 4-8; classical ballet, and tap and jazz for ages 7 and up.

Scott Boyer Teaches Dance 103 East Main Street 798-0945. Ballet, tap, jazz and pointe classes are offered.

Swift Creek Academy of the Performing Arts 2808 Fox Chase Lane in Brandermill 744-2801. Jazz, ballet, tap, modern and street jam classes are offered amongst Swift Creek's many music lessons.

Theresa's School of Dance 545 Southlake Boulevard 379-9393. Children ages 2½ and up are taught ballet, tap, jazz and pointe.

West End Academy of Dance, Inc. 10620-C Patterson Avenue 740-0842. Ballet, jazz and tap are offered to children ages 3 and up.

Outdoor Performances and Free Concerts

There are first-rate concerts, plays or dance performances scheduled almost every evening from mid-June through August at Dogwood Dell and weekly presentations at other outdoor stages in every corner of Greater Richmond.

Come early, as good seats and close-in parking go quickly. Bring lawn chairs, mosquito repellent and a picnic supper. If you will be toting toddlers, forget the lawn chairs and picnic basket—opt for a blanket to sit on and lightweight snacks that take a long time to eat and fill up pre-concert lag time.

The "Big Gig" sponsored by Downtown Presents 643-2826. The city's biggest music festival runs every day for 2 weeks in mid-July, with concerts at the Carpenter Center, Brown's Island, VCU Performing Arts Center, Nina Abady Festival Park and assorted neighborhoods. "Music in the Garden," Lunchtime Live!," "Noon Tunes" and "Friday Cheers" are all a part of this exciting series. Watch for "Kids' Night Out" featuring big-name children's performers in concerts free for all children!

The Boulders Concert Series in the meadow on the lake at the Boulders 320-5500. This summer series of concerts attracts families with a diverse selection of musical entertainment plus activities for children. Vendors offer a variety of food and drinks.

The annual Fourth of July concert is held at the **Chesterfield County Courthouse Complex**. (See Seasonal Events)

Dogwood Dell Festival of the Arts Byrd Park Amphitheatre. Richmond Parks and Recreation Department sponsors a series of concerts, plays and musicals, featuring a variety of music that should accommodate everyone's taste. Sunday afternoons are highlighted with kids shows and picnics. The Fourth of July traditional fireworks, burst to the swells of the 1812 Overture and saluting cannons, are not to be missed.

Festival schedules available at libraries and Visitor Centers and published in newspapers.

Performing Arts and Festivities

Innsbrook After Hours 346-8528. Late Wednesday afternoon gigs at the Innsbrook Pavilion attract 20-, 30- and 40-somethings as well as kids, depending on which nationally known band is jamming that day. Children under 12 are free, and many activities geared for children are available. The weekly series starts in April and runs into September.

Life of Virginia Brookfield Concerts 6610 West Broad Street 281-6699. Free concerts on the lawn at Brookfield present nationally known as well as local performers in shows geared towards adults, though the early evening setting is pleasant enough for children.

The **Langley Tactical Air Command Band** plays patriotic music accompanied by a National Guard fly-over on the Fourth of July.

Peanut Butter 'N Jam Presents through the Children's Museum of Richmond 644-3288. This annual summer series features nationally known family entertainers and associated fun for children in a picnic-like setting.

Seasonal Events

The following scheduled events change slightly from year to year as far as when they occur. Many families have turned these annual events into honored traditions. Events are subject to change. We suggest, as always, to call first or watch for media announcements. Or contact the Virginia Division of Tourism, 901 East Byrd Street, Richmond, VA 23219 (786-2051).

January, February, March

Barn in Winter 358-7166. Maymont Park Children's Farm. Find out how the weather affects the animals and plants by spending a Saturday morning at the barn. Cat shows; dog shows; doll and toy shows; car, camper, RV and boat shows take place in early spring. Watch papers for announcements.

Junior League of Richmond's **"Read to Me at the Capitol"** features a spring afternoon reading of stories by various actors and local celebrities to stress the importance of reading to children.

Valentine's Day Party Valentine Museum 649-0711. Valentine and cookie decorating, movies and storytelling the weekend closest to February 14. Free.

Ringling Bros. & Barnum & Bailey Circus comes to the Richmond Coliseum for a week each year. Get tickets early. 780-4970.

NASCAR Pontiac Excitement 400 Winston Cup Series at the Richmond International Raceway. 345-7223.

St. Patrick's Day Parade 672-0158. As close to March 17th as possible, this Sunday event features clowns, floats, marching bands, horses and plenty of green. Previous parades have featured Irish Marching Children's Bands from the Republic of Ireland and Northern Ireland.

Children's Book Festival 355-7200. The Arts Council of Richmond throws this annual party each March in honor of reading. Storytellers spin tales, storybook characters come alive, and authors and illustrators make appearances to explain their talents and incite young imaginations. Free admission. Locations vary each year. Call the Arts Council for information regarding the location.

April and May

Azaleas in Bryan Park A marvelous display to walk or drive through. Papers announce when flowers are in full bloom.

Easter Parade Families in their Easter best stroll down Franklin Street from Belvidere to Third Street with various types of music on every block, roving performers and a children's activity area sponsored by Richmond Children's Museum. Sponsored by Downtown Presents, 643-2826.

May Fest Point of Rocks Park. Games, activities, arts and crafts show.

Performing Arts and Festivities

Azalea Festival Parade 233-2093. This event, timed to the first bursts of color from the now-native plant, begins at George Wythe High School and proceeds along Westover Hills Boulevard to Forest Hill Avenue, ending at Forest Hill Park. Featured are marching bands from all over the country, motorized units and equestrian teams.

Goochland Day Parade ending at Courthouse Green, followed by square dancing, bicycling and canoe racing, arts and crafts by children and amateur artists.

Virginia Horse Association Show at the Fairgrounds towards the end of April, 228-3238.

Day in the Park with a Friend Byrd Park 649-6325. Children meet police, fire and rescue workers. Demonstrations of fire and rescue equipment, canine and mounted units and helicopter jumps. Sponsored by the Richmond Times-Dispatch.

Arts in the Park Byrd Park 353-8198. Artists and craftsmen from the Eastern seaboard present woodcarvings, pottery, paintings, silver and copper jewelry, enamels, glass work, etc. Family-oriented show and sale occurring the first weekend in May.

Old-Fashioned Egg Hunt 672-5096. Toddlers to five year olds search for eggs at the Meadow Farm Museum. Registration required.

Annual Heritage Fair and Easter Egg Hunt with pony rides, entertainment, crafts and American and African-American history, at Poor Farm Park in Hanover, 798-8062.

Family Easter at Maymont 358-7166. This family festival is an exciting way to celebrate spring with music, games, egg hunt, crafts and some food at Maymont.

Earth Day 230-3950. This "day" has become a weekend event in Richmond, with events at the Carillon in Byrd Park and on Brown's Island. Besides regional bands, dance groups and entertainment aimed at children, kids and parents have a great opportunity to learn how to "think green" and start recycling through various activities, including an environmental scavenger hunt.

Village Green Fair Collegiate School 740-7077. Carnival activities, pony rides, country store, handcrafted items and food for sale, usually in April.

Kites for Kids 748-1130. This one-day event in April at the Coalfield Athletic Complex on Miners Trail Road will satisfy any kite fan with stunt kite demonstrations, kite contests, music and giveaways.

Daisy Days St. Catherine's School 288-2804. Games, family festivities, balloons, pony rides, refreshments, handmade items and plants for sale, usually the first Saturday in May.

Camptown Races Graymont Park is the site for this annual country horse race north of Ashland.

Strawberry Hill Wine and Roses Festival at the end of May features some children's activities plus food. 228-3217.

Greek Festival Greek Orthodox Cathedral 355-3687. This annual 4-day celebration features food, dancing and music; guided tours of the cathedral; arts and crafts for sale.

June, July and August

Ukrops/Target Family Jubilee 643-2826. This 20-year-old festival welcomes summer to the area with a lengthy day of visual and performing arts, food and drink. Focused on children and families, the event includes a series of hands-on areas presented by various sponsors which enable children to participate in performances and make crafts.

Dogwood Dell Festival of the Arts Byrd Park, June-August. Nightly concerts, dances, plays performed at Dogwood Dell amphitheater, free. Announced in local media. For other summer concert series, see Outdoor Concerts.

Family Craft Fair at Deep Run Park in early June, featuring an arts and crafts show, bands, children's activities, a petting zoo and more. 672-5134.

Virginia State Horse Show at Fairgrounds at Strawberry Hills, end of June. 228-3200.

Deep Run Horse Show at Deep Run Hunt Club Show Grounds, 3rd week of June. 784-9951.

Ashland Strawberry Faire In the heart of strawberry-picking time, the campus of Randolph-Macon College in Ashland is the site for the annual strawberry festival. Fresh strawberries galore, shortcake, strawberry lemonade, ice cream sundaes and more are offered to those attending amidst the many artisans and craftspersons displaying their wares. Free admission, supervised games and music make this a tasty treat for all!

Hanover Tomato Festival 752-6766. 100 arts and crafts; entertainment; children's showcase including clowns and performers, fire/rescue vehicle displays at Battlefield Park Elementary School. First or second Saturday in July.

4th of July Celebrated all over town with music, fireworks and activities:
Maymont Park and Meadow Farm/Crump Park have day-long celebrations with old-fashioned games, contests, patriotic music, living history, clowns, craft demonstrations, etc. (see Parks)
Fireworks display and 4th of July concerts at Byrd Park and Chesterfield Courthouse Complex. A band concert and National Guard fly-over at Brookfield (see Outdoor Concerts).

The "Big Gig" 643-2826. Two weeks of free concerts throughout the city with big and not-so-big names from all types of music. Admission for some performances. Sponsored by Downtown Presents.

Carytown Watermelon Festival 359-4645. Block party with watermelon eating contests, arts and crafts, music, clowns, etc.

James River Month This event started out as a fishing tournament and has turned into an exciting festival with wacky water fun for children. Snorkeling, history hikes, kids' fishing and more are all featured to teach the importance and fun associated with the James.

September

State Fair 228-3200. 10 days of carnival rides, games and sugar-coated delicacies from the midway, plus a petting zoo, concerts and animal-raising competition at Strawberry Hill.

Chesterfield County Fair Courthouse Complex 768-0148. Live shows, fireworks, rides, games, animals.

Rainbow of the Arts Rockwood Park 748-1130. Art show, entertainment and participatory activities all afternoon.

43rd Street Festival of the Arts at Forest Hill and 43rd Street 233-1758. Features music, crafts and a nearby playground filled with kids.

High on the Hog An annual block party in Church Hill's Libby Hill Park that could be the area's largest.

Second Street Festival turns back the clock to the 20's, 30's and 40's, when Second Street was the heart of Richmond's African-American community. Sponsored by Downtown Presents, 643-2826.

October

Richmond Children's Festival Byrd Park 355-7200. Best festival of the year for children. Nationally known performers sing and dance. Plenty of opportunities for children to get involved with sing-alongs, backyard circus, theater tent, dancing, magicians and storytelling. At craft tables, kids may take part in hundreds of creative activities. Most events are free. Food and refreshments. Sponsored by the Arts Council.

Performing Arts and Festivities

Southern States Autumn Harvest Festival Grand Illumination Parade on West Broad Street in October. 673-2177.

Fall Fun Day and Marathon Street Party Sponsored by Downtown Presents 643-2826. Children's activities, clowns, jugglers, crafts to make, etc. Free.

Field Day of the Past 741-3936. Steam engines; tractor pulls; antique cars, trucks and tractors; arts and crafts; rides; more. Admission. Rockville/Manakin-Sabot.

Harvest Festival at Meadow Farm Museum. This celebration of rural life features family-oriented activities, demonstrations and old-fashioned games and musical entertainment. Takes place the third Saturday in October.

November

Richmond Craft Show sponsored by Hand Workshop 353-0094. Juried arts and crafts featuring exhibitors from all over the United States. Special craft activities for children. Fee.

Model Railroad Show Science Museum. Model railroad enthusiasts bring their trains back to Broad Street Station with layouts and demonstrations. Admission included with entry to the Museum.

Joy from the World Science Museum 367-1013. International celebration of the winter solstice with over 22 nationalities displaying their home country's decorations. Trees are decorated with handmade ornaments. Cooking and craft demonstrations, music and dance. Runs from mid-November through New Year's Day.

December

Chanukah Festival and Concert 288-6091. The Jewish Community Center hosts this family concert.

Kwanzaa Festival 266-5428. The Ezibu Muntu African Dance Company features music and dance performances at the Richmond Centre.

Capital City Kwanzaa Festival 644-3900. The Elegba Folklore Society features storytelling, music and dance, as well as children's activities at the Arthur Ashe, Jr., Athletic Center.

Garden Fest of Lights Lewis Ginter Botanical Gardens 262-9887. An illuminated botanical and architectural tour throughout the gardens. Bloemendal House is also decorated botanically for the season! Small fee.

James River Boat Parade of Lights along the Appomattox and James River 751-INFO, ext. 458. Best view is from the Hopewell Yacht Club and public river frontage in Hopewell. It begins at the yacht club and ends in the James River.

Christmas

"The Nutcracker" 225-9000. The Richmond Ballet and the Richmond Symphony Orchestra present Tchaikovsky's holiday ballet. Several matinee and night performances at the Carpenter Center. Reservations recommended.

Nativity Play Carillon, Byrd Park. Every Christmas Eve, over 200 people, children to adults, present this colorful portrayal of the birth of Jesus. Carillon plays at 5:30pm, followed by play at 6pm. No charge.

Christmas in Court End 649-0711. The holiday season gets into full swing with festive performers at the Valentine Museum, John Marshall House, Museum of the Confederacy and St. John's Church.

Annual Yuletide Fest at the Meadow Farm Museum 672-5106. The annual presentation gives children an idea of how Christmas was celebrated in 1862.

Performing Arts and Festivities

A Yorktown Christmas 887-1776. Costumed interpreters explain children's games and crafts from more than 100 years ago. At the Yorktown Victory Center.

The **Grand Illumination** at the James Center and Shockoe Slip kicks off the Christmas shopping season.

Christmas Tours throughout many neighborhoods, including Jackson Ward and Church Hill as well as the official Fan Christmas House Tour.

Ukrops/Richmond Jaycees Christmas Parade begins at the Department of Motor Vehicles on Broad and moves east to Seventh Street, complete with giant helium balloons, marching bands, floats and a jolly Santa to end the parade. 559-6113.

"Amahl and the Night Visitors" 780-4213. This annual presentation is now at the Landmark Theater.

Christmas Open House at Maymont 358-7166. Celebrate an authentic Victorian Christmas complete with carolers, tour the Dooley Mansion, enjoy hot cider and take a carriage ride.

New Year's Eve

New Year's Eve Bash at the Richmond Children's Museum is an all-day series of events inside the museum, with something for everyone. With the price of museum admission. 643-KIDO.

Chapter 7

Neighbors

> **Petersburg**
> **Central Virginia**
> **Historic Triangle**
> **Tidewater**
> **Mountains**
> **Northern Neck**
> **Washington, D.C.**
> **Amusement Parks**

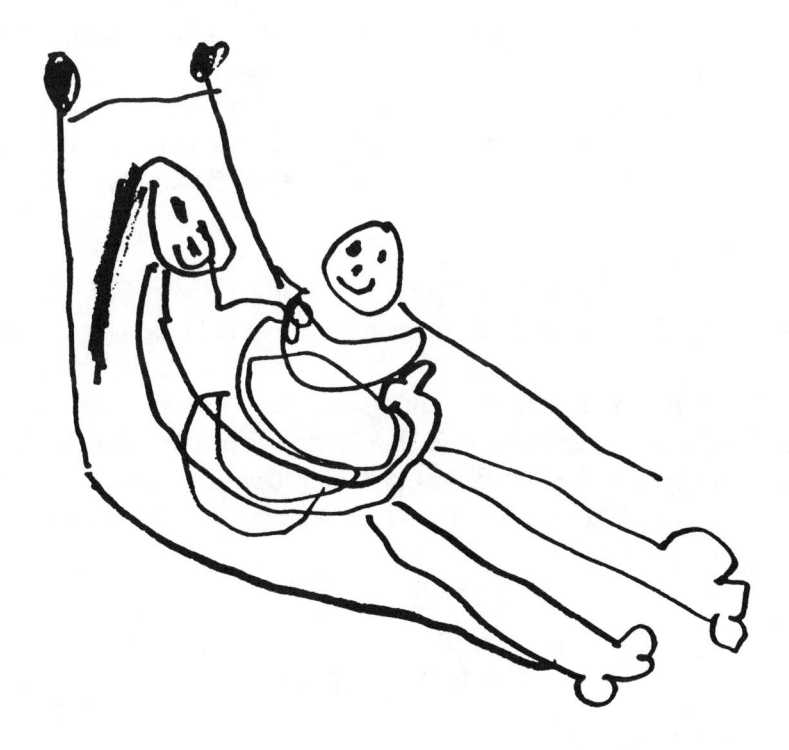

Kelsey Dwyer, Age 5
"My Baby and me at the beach"

Petersburg

Petersburg National Battlefield Visitor Center and Siege Museum 732-3531. On the site of this Civil War battlefield is the 170- by 60-foot crater, 30 feet deep, made by Union forces when they exploded four tons of powder in a tunnel dug beneath Confederate lines. Museum exhibits tell the story of the longest battle waged on American soil. Living history encampment in summertime. A self-guiding 4-hour tour of the battlefield is available at the center. Open daily 8am-5pm. $4.00 per person. Under 17 free.
 Directions: South on I-95, exit 52. East on Washington Street, follow signs.

United States Slo-Pitch Softball Association Hall of Fame Museum 3935 South Crater Road 733-1005. This organization sponsors numerous youth activities and runs this special museum featuring historical bat and ball displays, hundreds of action photos, and exhibits honoring the 63 current inductees. Guided tours available by appointment can be tailored to individual group needs and interests. Adults $2.00, students $1, under 10 free. Daily except holidays 9am-4pm, Saturday 10am-4pm, Sunday 12pm-4pm.

Old Blanford Church 733-2396. This early colonial building is an 18th-century parish church that became a memorial to the Southern soldiers who died during the Civil War. In honor of the Confederate dead, each of the eleven states of the Confederacy contributed a stained glass window designed by Louis Tiffany. This is also where the first Memorial Day was observed in June of 1866. Open daily 10am-5pm with tours every half hour. Adults $3.00, children 7-12 and seniors $2.00; children 6 and under are free.

Central Virginia

Flowerdew Hundred in Hopewell 541-8897. One of the earliest English settlements in the New World was located here. The museum displays artifacts recovered on this site dating from 9000 BC to the present.

A working 18th-century-style post windmill stands on the property. The annual Prince George County Heritage Fair is in April.

Open April through December 15. Hours Tuesday-Saturday 10am-4pm; Sunday 1-4pm. Closed Mondays. Adults $6; senior citizens $4; children 6-12 $3. Under 6 free.

Historic Triangle

Draw a line from Jamestown to Williamsburg to Yorktown and back to Jamestown, and you'll have the Historic Triangle. Take Route 5 from Richmond or take a scenic trip through plantation country along the James River. Another slow but interesting route is Route 10 through Hopewell, which includes a ferry ride at Scotland/Jamestown.

Colonial Williamsburg (800) HISTORY (447-8679). Restored capital city of Colonial Virginia. A national treasure, this is one of the largest and most complete projects of its type in the world, with 88 original buildings, over 100 acres of gardens, more than 225 exhibition rooms, and at least 17 crafts demonstrated by costumed staff. To enter buildings, one of three types of admission tickets is required:

- The Patriot's Pass – This is the best value, offering a year of unlimited admission to all Historic Area exhibition buildings and trade shops, daytime walking tours, Carter's Grove and three museums, as well as discounts on evening program tickets. $33 adults, $19 children ages 6-12, under 6 free.
- Basic Admission Ticket – A one-day ticket that offers admission to all Historic Area exhibition sites and trade shops (except the Governor's Palace) two museums and the orientation walk. $25 adults, $15 children ages 6-12, under 6 free.
- Colonist's Pass – Same as the basic ticket but good for two consecutive days as well as admission to Governor's Palace. $29 adults, $17 children ages 6-12, under 6 free.

Carriage rides are $6 per person, weather permitting. Reservations must be made same day at the Greenhow Lumber House on Duke of Gloucester Street across from Bruton Parish Church.

Williamsburg offers programs to delight children year-round and features many special hands-on activities, games and programs over holidays and summer vacation times. With any admission to Colonial Williamsburg, children can participate in the Children and Family Life Program. During summer months, young interpreters offer instruction in colonial games such as "trundling the hoop," stilt walking, jumping rope, lawn bowling, ninepins, leapfrog and blindman's bluff. At the rural trades site, children might help with basketmaking or seasonal chores such as hoeing or harvesting. Activities vary from day to day. For a complete listing of days, times and locations, consult the weekly "Visitor's Companion" when you arrive.

Colonial Williamsburg is open every day of the year, including all holidays; hours vary seasonally. The Colonial Williamsburg Visitor Center is accessible from I-64, exit 238. Just follow the green shield signs to Colonial Williamsburg.

Write for a free copy of the *Colonial Williamsburg Vacation Planner*, a glossy magazine with maps, motel accommodations and information, plus lists of annual programs, concerts, demonstrations and parades around which you might want to plan your trip. Colonial Williamsburg, PO Box 1776, Williamsburg, VA 23187. Or call 1-800-HISTORY.

College of William and Mary Sunken Garden Williamsburg. For children who are tired of all things colonial, the Sunken Garden is a great Frisbee-throwing spot as well as a nice place to picnic. The large "sunken" grassy field bordered by crepe myrtle and dogwood trees is located directly behind the Wren Building at the end of Duke of Gloucester Street. Pick up a picnic lunch at the Cheese Shop behind Merchant's Square.

Sir Christopher Wren Building William and Mary College (757) 221-1540. Located at the west end of Duke of Gloucester Street just past Merchant's Square, the Wren Building is the oldest college building in the United States. It has survived two wars and three fires and continues to be used by faculty and students. Guided tours conducted by William and Mary students are usually available when the college is in session. (One or more of the exhibition rooms may be unavailable for tours during official college functions.) Character interpreters from the Colonial Williamsburg Foundation make special appearances on occasion. Weekdays 10am-5pm; Saturday 9am-5pm; Sunday noon-5pm. Hours subject to change, particularly during college holidays. Closed New Year's Day, Thanksgiving and Christmas.

Yorktown Battlefield Visitor Center National Park Service (757) 898-3400. The Revolutionary War culminated in the battle fought at Yorktown in 1781, when Washington defeated Cornwallis and dashed the hopes of a British victory over the Americans. Browse through a museum with artifacts, dioramas and an observation deck. Rent an auto tape tour or see the battlefield by foot or bicycle, following the path across a bridge to Victory Monument and a view of the York River. Within walking distance of the village of Yorktown are many beautiful old, private homes. Public beach, picnicking and fishing areas are nearby. Daily 9am-5pm; extended hours in spring and fall. Adults $4, children 16 and under free.

Yorktown Victory Center (888) 593-4682, (757) 253-4838. Witness the birth of our nation at a museum of the American Revolution located in the town where independence was won in 1781. Innovative new exhibition galleries and an evocative film tell the story of the Revolutionary era from the perspective of ordinary men and women. Outdoors, take part in military drills and learn about 18th-century medical care in a living history Continental Army encampment. Visit costumed interpreters in a recreated farmsite of the late 1700s, with its herb and vegetable garden, crop field, log kitchen and tobacco barn. Open daily 9am-5pm; closed Christmas and New Year's Day. Allow at least two hours for a visit. Adults $7.25, children 6-12 $3.50.

Jamestown National Historic Site (757) 229-1733. Jamestown was the first permanent English settlement in the New World. The Visitor Center and Museum, operated by the National Park Service, is located at the edge of the original village site. View an introductory film, displays of excavated artifacts and a glass-making exhibit. A small bridge in the park crosses to Jamestown Island, kept in its natural wooded state—much as the colonists must have found it. Auto and walking tours are available at the center. Open daily except Christmas, hours vary seasonally. Adults $5, under 17 free.

Jamestown Settlement (888) 593-4682, (757) 253-4838. Next door to the National Historic Site, this living history park has life-size reproductions of the Jamestown settlement, Fort James, a Powhatan Indian village and the colonists' three ships—the *Susan Constant*, *Godspeed* and *Discovery*. Children of all ages will enjoy exploring the town and village, watching men and women dressed in costume going about the daily chores of 17th-century life in the wilderness, and talking with mariners on board the *Susan Constant*. Children of reading age will enjoy the exhibit buildings. Of particular interest is the documentary-style film which chronicles the life of a Jamestown colonist. Daily 9am-5pm. Closed Christmas and New Year's Day. Adults $9.75, children 6-12 $4.75, under 6 free. Combination tickets available for Yorktown Victory Center: Adults $13.25, children $6.50, under 6 free.

Jamestown-Scotland Wharf Ferry (800) VA-Ferry or (757) 294-3354. After your day at Jamestown, return to Richmond via the ferry, boarding at the end of Route 31. Bring bread to feed the sea gulls as you cross the James to Scotland Wharf. Ferry runs all year, about every half-hour, and it's free. Summer months are busy—you may have to wait. Stop at the Surrey House Restaurant for peanut soup and ham biscuits. It's inexpensive and relaxed.

Chippokes Plantation see State Parks.

Watermen's Museum on Water Street, Yorktown (757) 887-2641. This museum tells the story of the working watermen who ply the rivers and tributaries of the Chesapeake Bay. Boat models on display, as well as many exhibits that illustrate the skills used in crabbing, oystering and clamming. Outside, you can visit the workboats or try your hand at raising a sail or tonguing for oysters. Closed late December-April 1. Hours beginning April 2: 10am-4pm, Tuesday through Saturday; 1pm- 4pm on Sunday. Closed on Monday. Adults $3, students $1, children under 6 free.

U.S. Army Transportation Museum Fort Eustis (757) 878-1182. More than 200 years of transportation history—wagons, trucks, planes, helicopters, trains, boats, ships, amphibians, and even a flying saucer. Weekdays 9am-4pm, closed Mondays; Saturday and Sunday 9am-4:30pm. Free.

Tidewater

Nauticus One Waterside Drive, downtown Norfolk (757) 664-1000, (800) 664-1080. The National Maritime Center on the Virginia waterfront in Norfolk includes more than 150 hands-on exhibits, computer interactive games, AEGIS Command and the Nauticus Theater. Thrill seekers will especially enjoy petting a live shark in the touch pools.

The Hampton Roads Naval Museum located inside Nauticus explores 200 years of rich maritime history, and the Changing Gallery brings traveling exhibits from all over the world to the center.

The International Pier often hosts visiting ships from exotic lands. (Call to see which ships you can tour.)

Special rates available for group tours. School group programs also available. Summer hours: Memorial Day weekend through Labor Day 10am-5pm, 7 days a week. Fall and winter hours: Tuesday through Saturday 10am-5pm; Sunday noon-5pm.

Virginia Zoological Park 3500 Granby Street, Norfolk (757) 441-2706. Simulated natural environments in more than 53 wooded acres provide homes for over 350 domestic and exotic animals, including two rare white rhinos, African elephants, Siberian tigers and spider monkeys.

Accredited by the American Zoological Association, this outstanding zoo offers numerous programs for families as well as an extensive educational program for schools and groups. The "Zoo Snooze" lets children pack their sleeping bags and spend an evening at the zoo meeting touchable animals, making crafts and touring by flashlight. Saturday morning programs offer behind-the-scenes tours, crafts and hands-on activities for preschoolers and children 7-10.

"Zoopack: The Teacher's Guide to the Virginia Zoological Park" can be obtained by calling (757) 626-0803. This excellent resource offers tips for touring the zoo, information about each animal for teachers to share with their students, ideas for on-site activities, as well as pre- and post-visit activities. Open daily 10am-5pm. Closed holidays. Adults $3.50, children 11 and under $1.75; under 2 free. Free hour from 4-5 Sundays and Mondays. Additional fees for special programs.

Norfolk Botanical Garden Azalea Garden Road, Norfolk (757) 441-5830. Footpaths through world-class sunken Japanese gardens, rose gardens, a wildflower meadow and azalea court. The 155 acres are home to the International Azalea Festival. Boat tours run April through September, weather permitting. Train tours operate 10am-4pm mid-March through October. Open daily 9am-7pm April 15 through October 15; open 9am to 5pm October 16 through April 14. Small admission fee. Hands-on activities for children. Ask for an activity packet when you arrive.

Portsmouth Museums Downtown Portsmouth (757) 393-8983. Olde Town Portsmouth is one of America's most historic seaports, and this history is richly illustrated by the museums and landmarks along the waterfront: the Arts Center, Naval Shipyard Museum, Lightship Portsmouth. All are within walking distance. Admission to each is $1 per person; children under 2 are free. The Children's Museum of Virginia at 221 High Street, only a few blocks away, has more than 60 interactive exhibits based on the arts, sciences and the humanities. Be sure to visit the "bubble room" where you can enclose your whole body in a giant bubble. Admission is $4 per person; children under 2 are free. A "Key Pass" ($5 per person) provides entry to all four museums on the same day. Hours for all of these attractions are 10am-5pm Tuesday through Saturday; 1-5pm Sunday. The Children's Museum has Monday hours during the summer months.

Back Bay National Wildlife Refuge Virginia Beach (757) 721-2412. Known for waterfowl and shorebirds, with migrating Canadian geese in winter, this managed area features more than 7,000 acres of refuge for these wonderful birds. Visitor Center with decoy exhibits and "touch and feel" table for children. Center open daily, except holidays. Five miles south of Back Bay, check out False Cape State Park where you may see several types of turtles, whitetail deer, reptiles and more. For information about primitive camping at False Cape State Park call (757) 426-7128.

Grandview Nature Preserve State Park Drive, Hampton (757) 727-6347. This wildlife refuge and park offers walking trails and a beach you can get to only on foot.

Ocean Breeze Fun Park 849 General Booth Boulevard (757) 422-4444, (800) 678-WILD. This Virginia Beach site offers recreational activities for the whole family. Wild Water Rapids has a wave pool, tube rides, mat rides, children's areas and the new Paradise Pipeline. Motorworld has five race tracks of varying speeds, children's rides, golf, games and more.

Virginia Marine Science Museum 717 General Booth Boulevard, Virginia Beach (757) 437-4949, (757) 425-FISH. Explore the many fascinating creatures who make Virginia and its waters their home by participating in the entertaining and educational hands-on exhibits here at "Virginia's largest aquarium." See the tremendous 50,000-gallon aquarium. Meet artists carving duck decoys. The museum also offers seasonal whale watch boat trips. A fascinating experience for the whole family. The museum recently completed expansion and now houses the IMAX 3D Theater. Combination tickets which include admission to the museum and the IMAX 3D Theater prices are as follows: Adults $11.95, children 4-11 $9.95; children 3 and under free. Individual tickets are also available for the museum only. Prices for individual tickets are as follows: Adults $7.95, children 4-11 $5.95. The museum is open from Labor Day to Memorial Day 9am-5pm daily except Thanksgiving and Christmas. Summer hours are 9am-9pm.

The Goddard Space Flight Center Wallops Flight Facility (757) 824-1344. This important center showcases the past, present and future of flight with stories of Greek and Chinese flight continuing through the first space shuttle. Plenty of exhibits illustrate achievements in air and space travel including full-scale aircraft and rocket displays, a moon rock and displays of current and future NASA products. Model rocket demonstrations are conducted on the first Saturday of every month and third Saturday of June, July and August at 1pm. Daily puppet shows and special children's programs in the spring and fall; call for times. The Visitor Center is open 7 days a week during July and August. During the months of December, January and February, the facility is closed to the public but offers tours to special groups as requested. During the remainder of the year, the Visitor Center is open Thursday through Monday and closed every Tuesday and Wednesday. Admission is free. Handicapped accessible.

Mariners Museum Newport News (757) 596-2222. An international maritime museum featuring fabulous exhibits which trace over 3,000 years of maritime history. Walk among the international small craft collection featuring a gondola, a whaleboat, a sampan and racing yachts. Hand-carved, ornate figureheads and model ships crafted from metal, ivory and wood. On special occasions, ship modelers and wood-carvers are at work. Workings of a mirrored lighthouse lamp in operation. Picnic in the 500-acre shady park or rent a rowboat on Lake Maury. This is one of the best museums in the country and of interest to all ages. Open daily, 10am-5pm. Museum shop, park and research library admission as follows: Adults $6.50, students any age $3.25, children 5 and under free.

Casemate Museum Hampton (757) 727-3391. The cell which imprisoned Jefferson Davis after the Civil War and Civil War artifacts are on display at this museum housed in historic Fort Monroe. It is the largest stone fort in the country and the only operating fort with a moat around it. Focal point of museum is the U.S. Army Coast Artillery. Open daily, 10:30am-4:30pm. Free.

Hampton Carousel 602 Settlers Landing Road (757) 727-6347. This quick stop features a restored 1920s merry-go-round, open April through September, Monday-Saturday, 10am-8pm; Sunday noon-6pm. October through mid-December hours: Monday-Saturday 10am-6pm; Sunday noon-6pm. Closed mid-December through March.

Virginia Air and Space Center 600 Settlers Landing Road, Hampton (800) 296-0800. Just 45 minutes from Williamsburg, the center offers interactive exhibits, a historical perspective of NASA's accomplishments and the showing of exciting IMAX films in the center's 300-seat theater. You'll also find the Hampton Roads History Center located here. Summer hours are Monday through Wednesday 10am-5pm, Thursday through Sunday 10am-7pm. After Labor Day, Monday through Sunday 10am-5pm.

Virginia Living Museum 524 J. Clyde Morris Boulevard, Newport News (757) 595-1900. This museum is unlike any other found in Virginia, thanks to its mixture of the best features from a native wildlife park, science museum, aquarium, botanical preserve and planetarium. A living replica of the James River traces aquatic life in the river from the mountains to the sea. A two-story indoor aviary overlooking the lake houses dozens of songbirds native to Virginia, and an outdoor wetlands aviary is home to various heron and egrets, as well as numerous waterfowl. The outdoor nature trail around the lake and through the woods allows visitors to view the raccoon, beavers, river otters, fox, bobcat, deer and bald eagles in their natural habitat. The planetarium shows whisk viewers away to the planets and beyond.

During the summer months, the Virginia Living Museum often features "Dinamation" Dinosaurs outdoors in a jungle setting. These life-size replicas move and roar to the delight of dinosaur enthusiasts. (Call to verify times of the special attraction.)

Summer hours are Thursday-Saturday 9am-9pm, Sunday-Wednesday 9am-6pm. After Labor Day, Monday-Saturday 9am-5pm; Sunday noon-5pm and Thursday nights 7pm-9pm. Closed major holidays. Combination tickets, which include admission to the museum and planetarium, are $7 for adults and $5 for children ages 3-12. Student and special group rates available.

Cruises

Carrie B. Harbor Tours Portsmouth (757) 393-4735. An exact replica of a 19th-century Mississippi riverboat cruises past waterfront landmarks. You can see the nation's oldest working shipyard here. April-October and June to Labor Day. The cost of a 1½-hour tour is $9.95 for adults; the 2½-hour tour is $11.95 for adults. Children under 12 are half price for both tours.

Harbor Cruises Newport News (757) 245-1533. Tours Hampton Roads Harbor, Newport News Shipyard and Norfolk Naval Base. April-October.

American Rover Tallship Cruises Norfolk (757) 627-SAIL. Largest three-masted topsail passenger schooner under the U.S. flag tours the harbor from Waterside in Norfolk, early April through late October. Kids can get a chance to hoist the sails and learn some knots. One of American Rover's most popular programs are special educational field trips designed for students in marine biology, nautical history and seamanship, navigation, and/or ecology.

Tangier Island Cruises Chesapeake Bay (757) 891-2240. Cruise from Onancock one hour and 30 minutes to historic Tangier Island, discovered by Captain John Smith. This 700-resident island is accessible by boat or plane only. Villagers speak with an Elizabethan accent and make their living crabbing and harvesting oysters. May-October 15, 10am-4:15pm.

Mountains

Virginia Discovery Museum 524 East Main Street, Charlottesville 977-1025. Interaction is the key to this children's museum in the heart of downtown Charlottesville. Seasonal events and art programs are among the many activities designed for children and preteens. Special group rates available; reservations required.

Blue Ridge Parkway Asheville, NC, to Charlottesville VA. Historic attractions, scenic overlooks, picnicking, camping, resorts along 469 miles of scenic roadway through the George Washington National Forest. Open year-round, barring winter storms. Our favorite national campground and lodge is at Peaks of Otter in Bedford at milepost 84. The "Blue Ridge Parkway Directory" contains information on all commercial establishments, as well as mile-by-mile information on scenic and historic points of interest, folk art centers, picnicking, camping, hiking, etc. The "Parkway Milepost" is a newspaper printed three times per year with seasonal information. Call Parkway headquarters in Asheville (704-271-4779 ext. 245) for free copies and a map of the parkway.

Skyline Drive Waynesboro to Front Royal, VA (105 miles). Scenic road extends from the Blue Ridge Parkway through Shenandoah National Park to Front Royal. Toll per car $10. Maps and the park newspaper, *Shenandoah Overlook* (providing seasonal information about park activities) are available at the toll gates. To have information mailed to you, call Shenandoah National Park (540) 999-3500.

Visitor Centers at Dickey Ridge and Loft Mountain, as well as the Bird Visitor Center, offer a wide variety of programs, films and exhibits. Information about recreational fishing can be obtained at the toll gates and Visitor Centers.

For information about camping, lodging and reservations, upcoming activities and general park information, call (540) 999-3500. Big Meadows is a popular family campground, with an interesting mountain meadow to explore (lots of deer and blueberries), a beautiful nature center with exhibits, and activities for children. Must make camping reservations. Horseback riding available nearby at Skyland.

Skyline Caverns Route 340 South (540) 635-4545. There are numerous caverns in Virginia, but these, just beyond the Shenandoah National Park, are one of the only places in the world you can see anthodites, the slowest growing stalagmites and stalactites, taking 7,000 years to grow an inch. Here, you also find Rainbow Falls, which features a miniature train ride around the area. Open 9am-6:30pm in summer. Closes at 5pm in spring and fall and at 4pm in winter. Admission is $10 for adults, $5 for children 7-13; children under 6 are free with parents.

Montpelier just west of the town of Orange (540) 672-2728. Montpelier, the home of President James Madison and his wife Dolley, opened to the public in early 1987 and offers the satisfying feeling and enjoyment of discovering a new place not yet touched by the trappings of tourism. It is located on Route 20, near Orange, an easy scenic drive from Monticello in Charlottesville.

Admission includes a bus tour of the 2,700-acre estate and a tour of the mansion. Outside, a self-guided tree walk features more than forty species of trees from all over the world. A shuttle bus tours the grounds of the Madison estate, with its breathtaking view of the Blue Ridge Mountains, beautiful gardens and vast lawns, and the Madison family cemetery. Take along a picnic lunch!

Beginning in March 1998, after renovations are completed, visitors will enjoy a new audio system throughout the house and grounds, including archeological excavations on the property, as well as a new orientation video and new exhibits in the house.

Open daily March-December, 10am-4pm. Open weekends only in January and February.

Monticello Charlottesville 984-9822. Mountain-top plantation home of Thomas Jefferson, filled with his inventions and architectural innovations, personal mementos and period antiques. The house is often described as one of our country's foremost architectural masterpieces. Boxwood gardens, Jefferson's grave, craft demonstrations. Adults $9; children ages 6-11, $5. Daily 9am-4:30pm, except Christmas. March through October, 8am-5pm.

Northern Neck

George Washington's Birthplace Route 3, South of Colonial Beach 224-1732. This 18th-century working farm overlooking the Potomac River recreates life as it was in George Washington's time. Summertime craft demonstrations. Washington's birthday celebrated with wool-spinning, blacksmithing, period costumes, etc. Admission is $2 per person 17 & older (16 and under are free). Open daily 9am-5pm. Closed Christmas and New Year's Day.

Washington, DC

With so many wonderful museum, monuments, parks exhibits, historic sites and activities, where does one start? Our favorite for the D.C. area is **Going Places With Children**, compiled and published by the parents of Green Acres School, Rockville, MD. Includes a chapter called "Doing Washington in Three Days" for those on a limited time schedule, as well as everything from museums to parks, sports, entertainment, shopping, restaurants and businesses for those with many opportunities to come back. Send a check for $13.50 (includes tax and postage) to Green Acres School, Going Places, 11701 Danville Drive, Rockville, MD 20852 (301-881-4100).

Wolf Trap Farm Park (703) 255-1800. Nationally known for summertime performances by famous artists and resident professional companies, Wolf Trap is the only national park for the performing arts. More than 100 acres of wooded park surround indoor and outdoor performance centers. In mid-September, there is the International Children's Festival.

For information about free children's programs (Theater in the Woods), contact Wolf Trap Farm Park (703) 255-1827. Be sure to make reservations well in advance.

Reston Animal Park 1228 Hunter Mill Road, Vienna (703) 759-3636. This children's zoo allows visitors to feed and pet all types of exotic animals on its 56-acre lot. On special family nights, the Park offers pony rides, elephant rides and wagon rides. Weekend special events include arts and crafts, live animal shows and entertainers. Educational tours for school groups. Open from April to December.

Amusement Parks

Busch Gardens Williamsburg (757) 253-3350. Voted "Most Beautiful Theme Park" for the sixth consecutive year by the National Amusement Park Historical Association, Busch Gardens Williamsburg is a European-themed park with 17th-century flair. In addition to the world's top-rated roller coasters, Busch Gardens features eight mainstage productions, more than 35 thrilling rides and attractions, a wide variety of authentic foods and shops, and a children's adventure area. In 1997 Busch Gardens introduced "Alpengeist," the world's tallest and fastest inverted roller coaster at 195 feet and 67 mph.

Open weekends the end of March through mid-May with spring vacation week open as well. Mid-May through August, open 7 days a week. September and October, open Friday-Tuesday. Open at 10am each day.

Water Country USA Williamsburg (757) 229-9300. This 40-acre theme park, the largest water theme park in Virginia, offers exciting water rides, slides and entertainment—all set to a 1950s and 60s surf theme. A dark water ride combining the real-life adventure of white-water rafting with science-fiction fantasy was added in 1997. "Aquazoid" is the ultimate B-movie flashback. Game arcades, a sun deck, concessions and a picnic area. Showers and lockers are available. Open for weekends beginning in May, daily third week of May through Labor Day, and select weekends in September.

Paramount®'s Kings Dominion Doswell 876-5000. A 332-foot high replica of the Eiffel Tower offers a panoramic view of this huge family entertainment theme park. Favorite attractions include The Outer Limits™, Flight of Fear™ roller coaster, Nickelodeon® Splat City™, Days of Thunder® racing simulator, White Water Canyon raft ride and Hurricane Reef Water Park. Kidzville™, a town built just for kids, was introduced in 1997. Roller coaster fans will have a new mountain to conquer when Volcano: The Blast Coaster™ opens in the spring of 1998.

Open spring and fall weekends, Memorial Day-Labor Day daily.

Chapter 8

Working World

> Airports, Arts & Crafts, Banks, Farms & Greenhouses, Food Services, Media, Police/Fire Departments/Secret Service, Utilities, Weather Forecasting & Reporting

Graceann Pike, Age 4½
"Airplane"

Children are naturally interested in what adults do at work and are often surprised to find out how goods and services are provided to us. The following businesses and agencies welcome children in groups or with parents. This listing is just a beginning of the many places you might explore.

Airports

RIC Airport Tour Richmond International Airport 226-3076. Children go on an imaginary trip by plane when they tour the Richmond International Airport. The tour starts at the ticket counter, where they purchase imaginary tickets, and ends with the claiming of their pretend luggage at the baggage carousel. Children learn about airport security and travel safety. Whenever scheduling permits, groups also tour the inside of an airliner and meet the crew.

These tours are so popular they must be scheduled months in advance. Tours begin at 10:30am sharp Mondays through Thursdays and last 60 to 90 minutes. Maximum group size is 20, including adults.

FAA Tower Tour Richmond International Airport 222-7463. For an exciting, behind-the-scenes look at air traffic control and flight safety, tour the Federal Aviation Administration's control tower at Richmond International Airport. Tours are available by reservation only and are restricted to children aged 12 and older. Call for details.

Also tour the **Virginia Aviation Museum** at RIC airport. See listing under "Museums."

Aero Industries Richmond International Airport 222-7211. The public may observe small aircraft from a safe distance at Aero Industries, a local firm located near the Virginia Aviation Museum at RIC airport. Plane rides can be scheduled for a fee. Phone for details.

Arts and Crafts

In addition to being able to see works of art in the many local art galleries and museums, children have the opportunity to meet local artists and learn about their work firsthand. The following is a small sampling of those creative outlets.

Shockoe Bottom Art Center 2001 East Grace Street 643-7959. This converted warehouse near the center of historic Richmond provides the workspace for approximately 60 local artists. Families and small groups of children are invited to come tour the halls, meet the artists and get an eyeful of contemporary art in a variety of media. Not all of the artists are there all of the time. Hours for the public are Tuesday-Saturday, 10am-5pm. Call for details.

The Hand Workshop Art Center 1812 West Main Street 353-0094. The Hand Workshop is a combination of artists' studio, art school and gallery. It is one of the premier support organizations for craftspeople and has been a Richmond institution for more than 30 years. Children may tour studios and watch artists at work weaving, metal-smithing and throwing pottery. Tours for children aged 8 years and older may be reserved for a cost that includes an instructor's fee. Call for details.

The Hand Workshop also sponsors the T-N-T program for kids. T-N-T, which stands for "Teaching New Talent," is available after school hours and during the summer months. Children aged 8 to 16 years work with professional artists during week-long sessions. Programs include screen and block printing, bookbinding, stained glass design, designing and making jewelry, sculpture, pottery and more. Call for more information.

But Is It Art? 3031 West Cary Street 278-9112. Unlike the other listings, this is a retail shop and is not appropriate for groups. However, the shop is run as a cooperative venture and is staffed by the craftspeople who display there. When not busy helping customers, these artists will be happy to talk to children about their work and the creative process in general.

Banking

Federal Reserve Bank 701 East Byrd Street. The Federal Reserve Bank can be thought of as a bank's bank. It sets monetary policy and regulates the flow of money and credit into our economy. Richmond is the home of one of 12 Federal Reserve banks. Seated on the north bank of the James River, children will be amazed to learn that there is more of the building underground (where the vaults are) than in the 22 stories above ground.

Tours of the Federal Reserve Bank in action are restricted to families with older teens and to school classes of eleventh grade students and above. However, the Money Museum located on the ground floor is open to the general public without age restriction from 9:30am to 3:30pm Monday through Friday. (See Museums.)

Group tours of the Fed in action and the Money Museum are by appointment only. Call the Public Affairs Department at 697-8108.

Local Banks Branch Offices throughout metropolitan area. Children enamored of the things that money can buy may want to learn about the ways adults manage money through the use of bank services. And they may want to learn about career opportunities in banking, from teller to bank president. Area branch managers will be happy to answer their questions.

This activity is recommended for children aged 8 years old and older. Visits are by appointment only and may be arranged by phoning the public relations department at your favorite institution at least one week in advance.

Farms & Greenhouses

Children can learn about plants and the business of growing them by visiting local greenhouses and "pick-your-own" farms (see Chapter 4, "Pick-Your-Own Farms"). Make it an outing by seeking the answers to questions like these: What is the most unusual plant that grows in this area? Which plants need the most water? Which ones need the least water and why? What plants have red leaves? And how many different color "greens" are there? The employees of our local greenhouses can answer these questions and many others. Note that the greenhouses can be very hot in the summer.

The Great Big Greenhouse and Nursery 7139 Forest Hill Avenue 320-1317. Indoor and outdoor plants of many varieties, plus an extensive collection of tropical plants, are on display. Tours are given (except weekends and during the busy spring and Christmas sales seasons) by a knowledgeable employee. The 20-minute tour is recommended for children aged five to twelve years old. Call in advance to determine availability and make reservations. Families are invited to drop in at any time.

The Plant Man 3411 Kingsland Road 275-8919. The Plant Man grows all of the major holiday plants including Easter lilies and Christmas poinsettias. Employees will help students with science and nature projects on a time-available basis. Tours can be arranged by calling in advance.

Strange's Florist 3313 Mechanicsville Turnpike 321-2200. Tour the greenhouse and learn about an ecosystem. Learn how a greenhouse is constructed to trap heat and moisture and why this is vital to the business of growing plants. Strange's can handle a maximum group size of 25 children accompanied by adults. Call ahead to confirm staff availability.

Virginia Farm Bureau 12580 West Creek Parkway 784-1374. Hamburger doesn't come from McDonald's. Children who are not sure of this fact will want to experience the many programs available through the Virginia Farm Bureau's educational division. Call for details.

"Pick-Your-Own" Farms There are a number of "Pick-Your-Own" farms in the Richmond area, and all are fun to visit. For more information, see Chapter 4, Science and Nature.

Food Markets

Ukrops Supermarkets Main office: 379-7300. Locations throughout the metropolitan area. Children may visit all of the departments (meat, deli, produce and dairy) for a behind-the-scenes look at how a grocery store operates. Contact the manager at the store closest to you at least a week in advance to make reservations.

Ukrops offers older teens job opportunities from bagging to cashier. Call the employment office at 379-7301 for details.

17th Street Farmers Market 100 North 17th Street. Fresh farm produce is sold by growers in this famous market in the newly renovated section called Shockoe Bottom. There are 76 open-air stalls filled by farmers and generally a few craft vendors. Children can compare this alternative to their local grocery store, and ask the farmers questions. The market is usually open 6am-9pm from April to October, and sporadically during the winter months.

Media

Richmond Newspapers 333 East Grace Street 649-6900. Stop the presses! The newspaper still functions as a valuable news and entertainment resource in the age of instant telecommunications, online services and e-mail.

To see how a newspaper is produced and distributed, children over the age of ten are invited to visit the **Richmond Times-Dispatch**. Tours are available at both the Downtown Operations Center and at the Hanover Production Facility for groups of 5-30 children. Families will be considered as a small group. Visitors will see many of the steps in the production of the daily paper at both facilities.

Tours can be scheduled on Monday, Wednesday and Friday mornings, or on Thursday afternoons. Due to the popularity of the tours, please make arrangements one to two months in advance.

WWBT Channel 12 Television 5710 Midlothian Turnpike 230-1212. Take the video generation behind the scenes of this local NBC affiliate. The half-hour tour of the television station includes a 20-minute video that explains how the station operates, and a visit to the studio where the daily news broadcasts are produced. Children will have the opportunity to ask questions and view equipment. And if they are lucky, they might meet the on-air weatherperson or another local media celebrity.

Call well in advance to schedule a tour. The station can handle a maximum group size of 30 children accompanied by adults. Children must be 10 years of age or older.

Note that other local television stations have similar tour policies.

WCVE Channel 23 Public Television 23 Sesame Street. WCVE is not set up to accommodate regular tours of their facilities. However, they make up for this with their comprehensive educational outreach into the schools. Educators and scout leaders not already familiar with their programs can phone the office of Educational Services, 560-8133.

WRVA Talk Radio 200 North 22nd Street. Children in Richmond know WRVA as the radio station that is the first to report school closings on snow days. While they will not hear any rock and roll music (or any music for that matter) during their visit, they will see all key aspects of radio production. Tours are recommended for children aged 8 years and older, and require advance reservations. Due to the small size of the studios, groups of ten or less are preferred. For details, call Lou Dean at 780-3400.

WRVQ/Q94 3245 Basie Road 576-3200. Like most Richmond radio stations, WRVQ hosts visitors when reservations are made at least ten days in advance. Unlike Talk Radio, children will hear rock and roll music being played and have the chance to meet their favorite disk jockeys. Due to the small size of the studio, small groups are preferred. Larger groups may be divided as necessary.

Police, Fire Departments, Secret Service

The police and fire departments of all local municipalities (Richmond, Chesterfield and Henrico) offer a wide range of educational opportunities to the community. Part of their mission is to help children learn about the dangers they face and how to deal with them effectively. From stranger awareness to the importance of seat belts, from how to escape a fire to water safety, these programs cover the bases.

Most of the programs are designed to be taught to children in a class, scout troop or church group. However, as noted below, there are opportunities to visit a firehouse. Please note that, due to the fact they are required to respond to emergencies on a moment's notice, fire officials cannot guarantee their ability to keep appointments.

Parents are asked to follow these guidelines when requesting a program:

1) Call as far in advance as possible. McGruff (a canine character) and his pals Safety Pup, Dare Bear and Officer Remo (a remote-controlled talking police car) book up to a year in advance.
2) Make your event as regional as possible. If it is for a small Scout group, try to include other troops.
3) Check with the local elementary school to see if it is possible to incorporate your program into the school day to reach more children.

Henrico County Police Department 672-4821. Henrico offers programs that are structured to motivate children to learn how to take care of themselves and how to take responsibility for their own safety. The programs are presented in a non-threatening manner and explain how to make good decisions when faced with accidents, injuries and crime. Call for details.

Henrico County Department of Fire and Emergency Services Community Services Division 266-1916. Families and groups may tour any Henrico Country fire station by phoning the office of Community Service to set up an appointment. Tours last approximately an hour and children have the chance to ask questions. Please note that, due to the nature of the profession and the number of emergency calls that must be answered, the Fire Department cannot guarantee to be available for your group at the appointed time.

City of Richmond Police Department Office of Community Services 780-4632, or Juvenile Prevention Unit 780-5856. Drug resistance information, conflict resolution programs and street proofing programs are available for elementary schools. Call at least three weeks in advance to schedule.

City of Richmond Department of Fire and Emergency Services Support Services Division, 501 North 9th Street, Richmond, VA 23219 (780-4426). Tours of the firehouse, demonstrations of safety procedures and the opportunity to ask questions are available at the city fire station nearest you. However, requests must be made in writing three to four weeks in advance of the outing. Include the estimated size of your groups, dates you would like to tour, and a follow-up name and phone number. Requests may be mailed in care of the Support Services Division or faxed to 780-6671.

Chesterfield County Child Safety Programs 796-7051. Chesterfield offers a wide variety of tours and educational experiences, including tours of police facilities and the Safety Town program.

Chesterfield County Jail 748-1265. Tours are available. Children can visit the roll call room where officers check in, the court chambers, the old 1800s jail, and a state-of-the-art communications room. Call for details and reservations.

Chesterfield Safety Town 796-7051. Scout, church and school groups may visit Safety Town by making advance reservations. Safety Town is a mock village with streets, crossings, traffic lights and signs used to teach children about pedestrian and bicycle safety and stranger awareness. Call for details.

Chesterfield County Fire Department 748-1426. Tours of a Chesterfield firehouse are possible, with the understanding that emergency personnel cannot guarantee their availability. Groups can see a fire and safety film and hear an age-appropriate safety talk before touring the firehouse. Firefighters will answer questions and will bring equipment to special events (like safety and health fairs) on an equipment-available basis. Call a week or two in advance to make reservations. Groups are limited to 30 and should have at least one adult per 10 children. Families may visit on short notice by calling in advance.

United States Secret Service Special Agent in Charge, Suite 1910, 600 East Main Street, Richmond, VA 23219. The Secret Service does not offer tours. However, they will consider requests for a small group visit from children with a genuine interest in learning about the history of the Service, how it operates today and how a Presidential visit is handled. Requests must be made in writing and addressed to the Special Agent in Charge at the address above.

Utilities

How many Richmonders does it take to make a light bulb glow? Where does your bath water go when you open the drain? People who work providing us with basic utilities know the answers.

North Anna Nuclear Power Station Visitor Center, Mineral, VA (540) 894-4394. Tours are available. Call for information.
Surry Nuclear Power Station Visitor Center, Surry (757) 357-5410. Open 9am-4pm, Monday through Friday.

The North Anna facility lies about an hour northwest of Richmond, and the Surry plant is located about an hour southeast of town. Both offer the same educational exhibits documenting the development of commercial electricity from Edison's first experiments to nuclear generation. Emphasis is on nuclear energy. Trained information guides provide tours of the visitors' center and give lectures. Admission is free but reservations must be made.

Swift Creek Water Treatment Plant 13400 Hull Street 744-1360.
Proctor Wastewater Treatment Plant 748-7322.
City of Richmond Water Treatment Facility Maury Street Plant 780-7000.

All three plants offer a tour of the facility and a discussion of wastewater treatment. The tours are more interesting than they sound and fascinate children in grades four through seven. Make a reservation by calling in advance.

Weather Forecasting & Reporting

National Weather Service Wakefield, about an hour southeast of Richmond (757) 899-4200. The National Weather Service facility in Wakefield is a part of the national grid of weather centers that collects and interprets weather data and communicates the findings. Children will learn a great deal of weather science by visiting. Tours may be scheduled on Tuesdays and Thursdays by calling four weeks in advance for a group reservation. Tours are recommended for children aged 9 years and older. An advance request for a lecture to your group will be granted, schedule permitting.

NBC affiliate WWBT 230-1212
ABC affiliate WRIC 330-8888

At least two of the local television affiliates permit children to tour their facilities to learn how weather is reported. When scheduling permits, children might have the opportunity to meet their local weather personality. Call for reservations.

Shopping

Chapter 9

Shopping

Museum Shops, Books, Educational & Art Supplies, Toys, Hobbies, Used Clothing, New Clothing

Hunter Spangler, Age 4½
"Mommy and Daddy on the day they got married"

These are just a few of the many fine stores in our area known for the quality of their merchandise as well as for the friendly attitudes their shopkeepers exhibit toward children.

Museum Shops

Museum gift shops carry a variety of unique books and toys that you sometimes won't find anywhere else. There are large shops at the Virginia Museum and the Science Museum and the Maymont Emporium. Smaller shops at the Valentine Museum, St. John's Church and Chimborazo Park. (See Museums)

Books

Aquarian Bookshop 3519 Ellwood Avenue 353-5575. "New Age" and metaphysical books for children and adults, including music. Intriguing crystals on display and a cozy couch for relaxing.

The Baptist Bookstore 9840A West Broad Street, Glen Allen 23060 (965-9485). A full line of books. Supplies for church libraries. Good selection of children's music and tapes.

Barnes & Noble Bookstores
    1532 Parham Road 527-0051
    1601 Willow Lawn Drive 282-0781
    1200 Hugenot Road 378-3651.
This large chain features a huge selection of children's books and assorted items as well as regular story hours and activities.

Book People 536 Granite Avenue 288-4346. New and used books for children and adults. Special table and bench area for children to sit at to read their selections. The warm, friendly staff will do book searches to help you locate your childhood favorites to pass along to your special young person.

Books-A-Million
 8093 West Broad 270-1487
 9131 Midlothian 272-1792
This chain offers a complete line of hardcover and paperback books plus gifts, magazines, audio books, and much more.

Borders Books and Music 9750 West Broad Street 965-0733. Large children's selection including classics, board books, and adolescent literature. Separate area for children with a weekly story hour for preschoolers.

Cokesbury Books and Church Supplies 3700 West End Drive 270-1070. Good selection of children's books, including most classics.

Dave's Comics and Cards Village Shopping Center, 7019 Three Chopt Road 282-1211. Old and new comic books, baseball cards and card-collecting supplies. Richmond's traders' headquarters.

Edward T. Rabbitt & Co. Village Shopping Center, 7029 Three Chopt Road 288-2665. Cozy store with quality children's books, tapes and records and a helpful, friendly staff. Carpeted children's corner centers around a charming "tree," with many books and toys for kids while parent shops. An outstanding monthly storytelling hour for preschoolers.

Fountain Bookstore 1312 East Cary Street 788-1594. Many high quality classics, picture, board and beginner books. Highly selective collection. Convenient for parents working downtown.

Little Professor Book Center Bermuda Square Shopping Center, Chester 748-4352. Full selection of children's books, from board books to popular young adult novels and all the Newbery and Caldecott award winners. Also has books for the Young Virginian Readers Program. Back of store is for children, where they may sit and browse.

Logos Bookstore 716 West Grace Street 644-9924. Wide range of children's literature. Children's videos for rent, and a club "just for kids." Some religious titles. Cozy atmosphere with a wood-burning stove, video set-up, rocking horse, tables and chairs.

Narnia Children's Books 2927 West Cary Street 353-5675. Narnia, named after C.S. Lewis' famed children's series, "The Chronicles of Narnia," offers a select variety of books, tapes and records for children, adolescents, parents and teachers. The staff is knowledgeable and eager to help with special orders. Separate room for books on most any parenting or teaching topic. The store's newsletter reviews new books, announces children's events, visits by authors, upcoming workshops and store sales. Staff will also assist in compiling reading lists and organizing book fairs. Cozy "wardrobe" in back where children can curl up with books or toys while you shop.

Nostalgia Plus 1601 Willow Lawn Drive 282-5532. New and back-issue comics. Older children welcome to browse.

Richmond Book Shop 808 West Broad Street 644-9970. New, used and out-of-print books, including some children's titles.

Waldenbooks
   Cloverleaf Mall 276-8811
   Regency Square Mall 740-1253
   Virginia Center Commons 262-9479

Educational and Art Supplies

Art Market 1309 West Broad Street 353-7893. For a comprehensive selection of artist supplies, this is the place to go, especially if you know exactly what it is you want. College students frequent this store for art supplies.

Ben Franklin Crafts and Frames
    Willow Lawn Shopping Center 355-4900
    8524 Patterson Avenue 740-7306
    6610 Mechanicsville Turnpike 746-2832
    3500 Pump Road 364-2852

One of the largest selections of arts and crafts supplies in the area, with a variety of items for children and adults and a helpful, available staff. Children's craft classes on Saturdays as well as some summer sessions—children choose crafts of their interest and abilities. Class offerings vary. Some stores are available for children's birthday parties as well.

Hammett's Learning World
9663 West Broad 747-7808. Educational supplies, activities, games and educational toys, records, puzzles, stickers, art supplies. Duplicating materials and resource books for teachers. Workbooks for home use. Helpful staff are patient with children.

The Hobby Center
8908 Patterson Avenue 750-1973. If you're looking for something special for school projects, chances are, you'll find it here.

If It's Paper
    2413 Westwood Avenue 353-4175
    11417 Midlothian Turnpike 378-1988

Quantities of paper products at discount, party supplies, typing paper, magic markers, crayons, pencils, assorted sizes of cartons and boxes, arts and craft supplies—anything that's paper.

Main Art Supply and Framing
    1537 West Main Street 355-6151 (Art Supplies)
    1601 West Main Street 359-3499 (Frame Supplies)

Wide selection of professional and hobbyist art and framing supplies. Helpful staff will advise you as to the appropriate art supplies for children of various ages.

MJ Designs
    7580 West Broad Street 672-0203
    9744 Midlothian Turnpike 272-0031

These stores feature a great collection of arts and crafts projects, supplies and offer classes for kids and adults that utilize their products. You'll find a very helpful staff at both stores.

Tandy Leather Company 7526 West Broad Street 755-6716. This is a hobby shop for leather crafts. Kits for wallets, key chains, belts and other leather items for a diversity of skills levels.

Teach 'N' Things
    11101 Midlothian Turnpike 379-0647
    7107 Staples Mill Road 262-1395

Teachers' supplies, idea books for parents and teachers, educational toys, workbooks, games and puzzles, arts and craft supplies, Sunday School materials, stickers.

Toys

Bears 'n More 3004 Stony Point Shopping Center 323-7550. Specialty stuffed animal store. Great selection of every possible animal around.

Beck & Little 3007 West Cary Street 355-3030. Long-time favorite of kite enthusiasts, featuring a good selection of kites, windsocks, golf discs and other flying toys.

The Disney Store
    Regency Square 740-8034
    Virginia Center Commons 261-1930

Toys and clothing all associated with Disney movies and memorabilia. Also carry many Disney collector items. Stores have a large-screen TV for children to watch all their favorite Disney videos while you shop.

Shopping

The Great Train Store Regency Square Mall 740-2059. Specialty store carrying train books, videos, and preschool train toys to adult train toys and collectibles. Excellent selection and knowledgeable staff.

Kay-Bee Toys
   Regency Square Mall 740-7058
   Fairfield Commons Mall 222-4063
   Chesterfield Towne Center 379-2281
   Clover Leaf Mall 276-9225
   Willow Lawn Shopping Center 285-3026
Good selection of toys, games, puzzles, dolls, models, trains and some arts and craft supplies.

Kidkadoo, Inc. Virginia Center Commons 264-8970. Specialty toy store featuring many educational and high quality toys

Kidpourri 1601 Willow Lawn Drive 282-0750.

Paddington Station 10450 Ridgefield Parkway 741-4772.

School Crossing Harbour Point Shopping Center 639-1879. Toys designed to educate and entertain. Also carry educational software.

Shenanigans 6233 River Road Shopping Center 673-4528. Specialty toy store carrying high quality and unusual toys.

Toy Center 5811 Patterson Avenue 288-4475, 288-7345. Quality toys, collector dolls, miniatures, dollhouse building materials and furniture, party favors, books, arts and crafts supplies, European toys. An elaborate train board is visible from outside display window.

The Toymaker of Williamsburg Shockoe Slip 1215 East Cary Street 783-1744. Highly selective collection of fine toys, including many imported and stuffed animals, as well as books.

The Toy Shoppe 11632 Busy Street 379-2138, 794-6333. Large selection of educational and developmental toys and gifts to fascinate and challenge, including European toys, dolls, and wooden play yard equipment. Also videotapes and music. Even toys for children to play with while you shop. Staff helpful and friendly.

Toys-R-Us
   7545 Midlothian Turnpike 276-1544.
   8700 Quiocassin Road 740-6116.
Floor-to-ceiling toys, sporting goods, bicycles, records and tapes, games and puzzles, infant clothing and equipment, discount disposable diapers. These are huge stores.

Toys That Teach
   Gayton Crossing 1340 Gaskins Road 741-5611.
   Stony Point Shopping Center, 3020 Stony Point Road 272-2391.
Fun, educational toys of quality, both American and European; books and tapes; some craft supplies. Helpful staff.

Toys, Trains & Teddy Bears 1003 Sycamore Square Drive 378-8697. Collectible trains, dolls, teddy bears, etc. High quality line of products.

Hobbies

Bobby's Toy Trains 32 Broad Street Road, Manakin-Sabot 784-4473. If you're looking for anything related to model railroading, check out Bobby's first.

Bob's Hobbies & Raceway Mechanicsville 746-2758. A great collection of radio-controlled cars, helicopters, boats and airplanes.

Chesterfield Hobbies Village Marketplace, 13154 Midlothian Turnpike 379-9091. This store offers a full line of hobbies, from model railroading to rockets and cars.

Frances' Stones 13101 Spring Run Road, Midlothian 739-3981. Large collection of geodes, agates, fossils, semi-precious stones (cut and

Shopping

uncut), crystals, petrified wood, arrowheads, sharks' teeth, rock hound supplies and many guidebooks.

The Hobby Center, Inc. 8908 Patterson Avenue 750-1973. Model cars, planes, boats, rockets, trains and plastic models for ages 8 and up, since 1956.

The Hobby Corner 7150 Hull Street Road 276-4151. This hobbyists' delight specializes in radio-control vehicles and trains.

Packard's Stamp and Rock Shop 13131 Midlothian Turnpike 794-5538. An array of Virginia minerals and fossils, worldwide mineral specimens, semi-precious stones and gems and finished jewelry. Displays in low glass cases for easy (out-of-reach) viewing. A full line of rock hound supplies—cutting equipment, mounting supplies, mineral kits, hobby books, maps, collecting guides. Prices range from a number of inexpensive curiosities like sharks' teeth, medium-range geodes and fossils, to valuable collectors' items.

The Great Train Store (see entry under "Toys")

Used Clothing

The Butterfly Consignment Boutique 5726B Patterson Avenue 288-4700. Good quality used clothing for children and adults.

Children's Market and Exchange 2926 West Cary Street 359-6950. A bright store featuring children's resale clothing, furniture and toys. New clothing, including many brand names, available at a discount.

The Hall Tree 12 South Thompson Street 358-9985. Consignment shop selling maternity, children's, infant's, men's and women's wear. Also some jewelry and accessories.

Nanny's Kids 12345 Gayton Road 754-0185. Good selection of children's clothes and accessories.

New 4 U Genito Crossing Shopping Center 763-2409. Good quality children's, ladies', men's and maternity apparel.

Once Upon a Child 9111 Midlothian Turnpike 272-2229. Clothing, furniture and anything else related to children can be found here. Consignors are paid for their items when they are brought in rather than when they are sold, as in traditional consignment stores.

My Sister's Closet 10478 Ridgefield Parkway 754-2127.
Private Collections Oxbridge Square 674-1993.
Rainbow Collection 13337 Midlothian Turnpike 794-2168.
Sassy Consignments 11101 Midlothian Turnpike 379-5651.
2nd Time Around Consignment, Inc. 600 England Street 798-1410.
Sheila's from the Top 6788 Forest Hill Avenue 272-8009.
Sisters Four, Ltd. 9940 Midlothian Turnpike 330-3730.
Wardrobe Exchange 10619 Patterson Avenue 740-4017.

All of the above are good quality consignment stores with ranging selections of children's clothing, shoes, toys, etc., as well as adult wear. Call for specific items that you may be looking for.

New Clothing

Annette Dean Kids Wear 3325 West Cary Street 359-8240. Infant-Girls to size 14, Boys to size 20. Very stylish, excellent quality.

Buttons & Bows 8905 Three Chopt Road 285-0482. Heirloom clothes and smocking supplies and classes. Custom-made clothing. Many classic, special occasion clothes and accessories. One of Richmond's traditions.

The Children's Place Chesterfield Towne Center 379-9110. Infants to size 14, selling quality clothing. Plus a children's play area.

Children's Wear Digest Co. Store Ridge Shopping Center 282-6887. Large selection of brand name as well as classic-type children's clothing. Some infant accessories. High quality.

CWD Outlet 1368 Gaskins Road 740-0192. Classic children's clothing, high quality wear; all at reduced prices.

Gap Kids
  Regency Square 740-0216.
  Chesterfield Towne Center 379-9896.
  Virginia Center Commons 262-5473.
Nationwide children's retail store carrying high quality clothing and accessories.

Gymboree
  Regency Square 740-0172.
  Chesterfield Towne Center 378-7892.
Nationwide children's retail store featuring brightly colored children's wear. Toys and accessories available as well. Full-screen television in store, with children's tapes featuring "Gymbo the Clown."

Kids-R-Us 7300 Midlothian Turnpike 745-2678.

Milby's Just Kids
  Meadowbrook Plaza 275-8384.
  Stony Point Shopping Center 330-8158.
Both shops carry infant to girls and boys size 14. Specializing in pageant-wedding-cotillion apparel.

Who's That Kid? Belle Grade Shopping Center 378-2398. Unique, superior quality children's clothing.

Richmond Is for Children

Chapter 10

Kids and the Internet

> **Local and State Interest**
> **Colleges and Universities**
> **Public Radio and TV**
> **Newspapers and Magazines**
> **Museums**
> **Education Resources for Kids and Parents**

Carolyn Pelnik, Age 6
"The computer"

You can find lots of great kids' stuff on the Internet or World Wide Web. If you don't know what the web is, check with your local library branch, your favorite computer whiz or just ask your kids; chances are, they'll know. In this chapter, we'll mention some places to start for great stuff in the Richmond area and of interest to kids and parents. Information on the web is growing so fast that no book could possibly stay current, but if you start with some of these sites, you will soon find yourself stumbling across an immense variety of great information. In the listings that follow, we give an abbreviated web address. For the full address, simply type "http://" and then the address given in the text. Just remember that on some kinds of computers, capitalization counts. Type slowly and carefully; for computers, close is just not there.

Local and State Interest

A great place to explore Richmond on the web is the **Insider's Guide to Greater Richmond** (www.insiders.com/richmond-va/index.htm). You can find lots of basic, useful information about the Richmond area at this site.

Another good path to local information is the **Commonwealth of Virginia** homepage (www.state.va.us). From here you can find links to state government agencies, the Virginia Library and lots more.

Among the agencies, check out the pages for the **Department of Conservation and Recreation** for information about parks. The **Department of Agriculture** has information about Christmas trees, pick-your-own fruits and vegetables, and Virginia food festivals (www.state.va.us/~vdacs/opms/opmsbrc1.htm).

Of special interest is the page full of links to local governments. All nearby cities and counties have links here (www.state.va.us/home/arolocal.html).

Or try **Visit Virginia** for a guided tour of state attractions in any of five languages (www.virginia.org). This site offers brochures, discount coupons, weather information and more.

Colleges and Universities

Area colleges and universities have extensive web resources. Most schools put their events calendar and course schedule on a web page. And while we're on the subject of college, if you ever wondered how you were going to afford such a thing for your kids, check out the **Prepaid Education Program** of the Virginia Higher Education Tuition Trust Fund (www.schev.edu/wufinaid/vhettf.html).

University of Richmond www.richmond.edu
University of Virginia www.virginia.edu
Virginia Commonwealth University www.vcu.edu
Virginia State University www.vsu.edu
J. Sargent Reyolds Community College www.jsr.cc.va.us

Virginia Union University did not have a website at the time this guide was published.

Public Radio and TV

You'll find lots of interesting information at the site for public radio and TV (www.wcve.org). The information includes upcoming programs, community events, web addresses and e-mail addresses for staying in touch with all your favorite shows. You'll find links to National Public Radio and the Public Broadcasting System.

On the public radio side, the "Family" page includes information on Rocket Radio and on Rabbit Ears Radio. The public TV pages include links to Mr. Rogers' Neighborhood, Bill Nye: The Science Guy, Nature, Newton's Apple, Lamb Chop, Nova, Shining Time Station, Reading Rainbow and much more.

Newspapers and Magazines

Items of local interest may be found at the sites of local newspapers and magazines.

Start with **Media General's Gateway Virginia** (www.gateway-va.com). After you've scanned the news and sports, try the "Gateway Guides" to the Richmond area as well as to Washington D.C., Williamsburg, the Chesapeake Bay, and the Blue Ridge.

Style Weekly magazine's address is www.styleweekly.com

Museums

For an up-to-date list of the websites of many of the museums in Virginia, visit the website of the **Virginia Association of Museums** (xroads.virginia.edu/~VAM). This site is operated by the American Studies Group at the University of Virginia.

Another resource is **Virginia Museums: A Guide** (www.comet.net/MUSEUMS).

The **Children's Museum of Richmond** is now on the web at (www.cmorich.org). You'll find all the most up-to-date information on the Children's Museum here, plus links to other sites of interest to children and their parents. Don't miss it!

The **Science Museum of Virginia** is easy to find (www.smv.mus.va.us). Find information on the latest comet, eclipse or Omnimax movie here. This site always contains links to other great science resources.

There's a lot to see at the web page for the **Virginia Museum of Fine Arts** (www.state.va.us/vmfa/index.html). Aside from information about current and future exhibits, you can find lists of their classes for children as well as links to other art websites.

Definitely try the **Virginia Museum of Natural History** homepage (www.vmnh.org). The bug-of-the-day is too good to miss. Or try the dino-link, or critters, or just "Cool!." You won't be disappointed. You can even get access to Dr. Michael Kosztarab's opus: *Scale Insects of Northeastern North America: Identification, Biology, and Distribution.* Curl up with that one…

For you Civil War buffs, don't miss the **Museum of the Confederacy** homepage (www.moc.org).

The **Mariners Museum** in Newport News has information on all things that float on the ocean and the people who love them (www.mariner.org).

Additional Museum "surfing" that you might try:

> **Virginia Historical Society** (http://www.vahistorical.org)
> **Monticello** (http://www.monticello.org)
> **Colonial Williamsburg Foundation** (http://www.history.org)
> **Valentine Museum** (http://www.valentinemuseum.com).

Education Resources for Kids and Parents

The array of educational resources available on the web is astonishing. No matter what your area of interest, it's out there. Arts and arithmetic, science and space, zoos and ZIA. You can dissect frogs on-line or learn all about chocolate. These listings are not limited to Richmond or even Virginia, although Virginia is doing some very good things on the web. Here are a few of the best entry points to educational resources on the web.

Start with the **ERIC Clearinghouse on Elementary and Early Childhood Education** at the University of Illinois (ericps.ed.uiuc.edu). This gives you access to the ERIC education database plus special collections on important special topics such as the Reggio Emilio Approach, the Project Approach and more. There are links to lots of other resources on the web.

Virginians should be proud of the **Virginia Public Education Network** (pen.k12.va.us) Arts, science, geography; resources for educators, parents and children.

The **Virtual Schoolhouse"** (sunsite.unc.edu/cisco/index.html) contains a large repository of educational resources of all kinds.

The Virginia Society for Technology in Education hosts its **"Yellow Pages for Online Educators"** (www.bev.net/education/schools/admin/vste-sites.html).

The University of Minnesota College of Education and Human Development publishes **Web66** (web66.coled.umn.edu) to help educators set up web servers, to link K-12 schools and to help K-12 programs find the information they need.

Another list of **educational resources** on the web can be found at www.infi.net/~wsg/educ.html.

Melanet's **"Watoto World"** is a website for children, parents and educators of African descent. (www.melanet.com/watoto/watoto.html)

For resources on the teaching of math and science, try these:

> **National Science Teachers Association** (www.nsta.org)
> **National Council of Teachers of Mathematics** (www.nctm.org),
> **Annenberg Foundation and Corporation for Public Broadcasting Math and Science Project** (www.learner.org/content/K12).

Appendix

Appendix

Recreation Centers and Organizations
Libraries
Recreational Opportunities for the Handicapped
Summer Camps
Parenting Centers

Cooper Guncheon, Age 6½
"Skateboarding"

Recreation Centers and Organizations

B'nai B'rith Organization 5403 Monument Avenue 282-4174. Social youth group for Jewish teens in grades 9-12, focusing on leadership training.

Boys & Girls Clubs of Richmond
  408 North Robinson Street 353-3246
  West End unit, 910 South Harrison Street 359-1824
  Southside unit, 2409 Bainbridge Street 230-0757
  Blackwell Unit, 214 East 13th Street 231-0352
  Teen Center (age 13-18) 910 South Harrison Street 359-8573

For boys and girls ages 7 to 17. Game room with ping-pong and video games, indoor swimming pool, library with computers. Programs in arts and crafts, drama and music, photography. Summer camps. Annual dues.

Boy Scouts of America 4015 Fitzhugh Avenue 355-4306. Scouting begins at age 6 with the Tiger Cubs, Cub Scouting for ages 6-8, and Boy Scouts for ages 8-18, with the goals of character development, mental, emotional and physical fitness and good citizenship. Summer camp. Annual dues.

Commonwealth Girl Scout Council of Virginia, Inc. 7300 Hanover Green Drive, Mechanicsville 746-0590, (800) 4-SCOUT-4. Helping girls make friends, serve the community and develop their potential. Girls begin at age 5 in Daisies; Brownies, ages 6-8; Junior, 9-11; Cadettes, 12-14; and Seniors, 15-17. Summer camp. Annual dues.

Jewish Community Center 5403 Monument Avenue 288-6091. Recreational programs for members as well as the community. For preschoolers who are members there is pottery, puppetry, drawing and painting, cooking, piano, and computer classes. Non-member classes include soccer, wrestling, gymnastics, tumbling and karate. There is an outdoor activity program for grades 3-7. An after school program is available for elementary-age children with membership. Transportation provided from area schools. For members, there is swimming, tennis, racquetball, a fitness center, a health club and other activities. Everyone is welcome.

Presbyterian School of Christian Education 1205 Palmyra Avenue 359-5031. Craft classes for preschoolers through teens, including pottery-painting, metal-tooling, basketry, holiday crafts and music lessons, many at no cost.

Salvation Army Boys & Girls Club & Neighborhood Center 3701 R Street 222-3122. After school programs including swimming, gymnastics, softball, arts and crafts, computer courses for boys and girls ages 6-18. Open Saturdays, closed Sundays and Mondays. Annual fee.

Young Men's Christian Association of Greater Richmond Area YMCAs provide a variety of programs and activities for all ages, including team sports—volleyball, soccer, baseball, T-ball—and individual sports—gymnastics, karate, swimming, fitness and aerobics among others. The nine YMCAs are

- Chester, 3011 West Hundred Road 748-9622
- Chickahominy, 5401 Whiteside Road, Sandston 737-9622
- Downtown, 2 West Franklin Street 644-9622
- Manchester, 7540 Hull Street Road 276-9622
- Midlothian, 2737 Coalfield Road 379-5668
- North Richmond, 4207 Old Brook Road, near Ginter Park 329-9622
- Patrick Henry, 405 England Street, Ashland 798-0057
- Shady Grove, 4024-C Cox Road, Glen Allen 270-3866
- Tuckahoe, 9211 Patterson Avenue 740-9622
- Metropolitan Office 649-9622.

YWCA 6 North Fifth Street 643-6761. A variety of sports and activities for all ages. Child care and after school programs here.

City of Richmond Community Centers There are more than 30 Community Centers and a number of playgrounds located throughout the city with programs and activities for all ages. Youth sports include basketball, baseball, football, soccer, indoor and outdoor swimming and gymnastics. Many centers have supervised playground programs open in the summer until dark and after school, fall and winter. Children can drop in for activities or sign up for the many programs going on, including arts and crafts and a city-wide youth ballet program that is free.

- Battery Park, 2803 Dupont Circle 780-8144
- Bellemeade Community Center, 1800 Lynnhaven Avenue 780-5035
- Blackwell-Maury, 14th and Maury Streets 780-5081
- Broad Rock, 4615 Ferguson Lane 780-5399
- Humphery Calder, Stuart Avenue and Thompson Street 780-8780
- Chimborazo, 30th and East Marshall Streets 780-4603
- Calhoun Community Center, 436 Calhoun Street 780-4403
- Creighton Court, 2101 Creighton Road 780-4425
- Fairfield Court, 2506 Phaup Street 780-8649
- Fisher, 3701 Garden Road 323-3075
- J.L. Francis, 5146 Snead Road 276-8009
- Alice Fitz Playground, 13th and Penny Streets 233-5359
- Franklin Community Center/Fonticello Playfield, 3100 Midlothian Turnpike, 28th and Bainbridge Streets 780-5027
- William Fox, 2300 Hanover Avenue 780-6011
- Highland Park Plaza/Providence Park Playground-Carolina Avenue and Pollock Street, 460 East Ladies Mile Road 329-6450
- Hillside Court, 1500 Harwood Street 780-5398
- Holly Street Playground, Laurel and Holly Streets 780-4505
- Hotchkiss Field, 701 East Brookland Park Boulevard 780-4466
- Maymont, 1211 South Allen Avenue 780-6847 or 780-8609
- Mosby, 1000 Mosby Street 780-4511
- Pine Camp, 4901 Old Brook Road 264-2898
- Powhatan, 1000 Williamsburg Road 780-8583
- Randolph, 1491 Grayland Avenue 780-6227

G.H. Reid/Elkhardt Community Center, 1301 Whitehead Road 276-7247

Bill Robinson, 701 North 37th Street 780-4053

Rueger/Byrd Park/Cary Community Center, Maplewood Avenue and Sheppard Street 780-6266.

Thomas B. Smith, (formerly Ruffin Road) Community Center 2015 Ruffin Road 780-5090

Thompson/Huguenot, 7825 Forest Hill Avenue 320-3717

Westhampton, 5800 Patterson Avenue 285-1416

Whitcomb Court, 2302 Carmine Street 780-8021

Westover, 1391 Jahnke Road 780-5095.

Henrico County Parks and Recreation Ten recreation centers are open September to May with morning playground activities, extended day recreation programs and day camp in the summertime. The general information number is 672-5100.

Year-round activities for all ages include arts, crafts, dance, music, sports, drama, computers and nature, also teen programs and a teen theater company. The county sponsors over 90 different leagues of baseball, softball, basketball, soccer, football, tennis, rugby and gymnastics. Expeditions for all ages have included in the past Luray Caverns, Washington D.C., and Williamsburg.

For special populations there are tenpin bowling tournaments, family activities, folk dancing, creative movement and craft workshops.

The county sponsors an after school program for Henrico children at a number of elementary schools in the county Monday-Friday, arts and crafts, games, music, dance.

For preschoolers, ages 3-5, Kiddie Kollege provides opportunities for fun and socialization. Other programs are offered occasionally for mothers and tots.

Reserve picnic shelters five days in advance, March-December. Picnic kits including bats and balls, horseshoes, volleyball and badminton equipment, etc., are available. For rental, call 672-5094.

Schedules of upcoming programs, classes and events can be found at library branches, or contact 672-5102.

Recreation Centers:

  Belmont Park, 1600 Hilliard, 262-4728
  Confederate Hills, 302 Lee Avenue 737-2859
  Dorey, 7200 Dorey Park Drive 795-2334
  Varina, 8081 Recreation Road 795-1837

Community Centers:

  Central Gardens, 2401 Harman Street 780-1009
  Gravel Hill, 5417 Longbridge Road 795-5727
  Highland Springs, South Ivy Street 328-0480
  Sandston, 11 J.B. Finley Street 737-3972

Chesterfield County Parks and Recreation Chesterfield County's many spacious athletic facilities and playgrounds are completed by undeveloped forests and meadows with nature centers and trails. The Parks and Recreation Department focuses its activities on nature awareness and natural and cultural history as well as team and individual sports.

For five to twelve year olds, there is the Junior Naturalist Program. Short hikes combined with craft activities help deepen a child's understanding of the outdoors. Children might make paper or animal track castings or learn to tell what type of food a bird eats by its beak and feet.

The Adventure Team offers outdoor activities year-round for ages 13-18. Past excursions have included archaeological digs; spelunking in Virginia's caves; rock climbing (both co-ed trips and women only); fundamentals of canoeing, kayaking and sailing; and scuba diving. Many of the workshops are free; there are fees for the weekend excursions.

For families, groups and individuals there are short hikes on Saturday and Sunday mornings.

Other children's activities include creative movement, exercises, music and dance for ages 3-5 and an instructional baseball league (ages 7-12), emphasis on fun rather than winning. Also offered are several therapeutic recreation programs.

The county sponsors many "living history" events such as the Civil War "muster" at Point of Rocks and a costumed reenactment of the founding of Henricus in the fall.

Picnic shelters can be reserved after January 1 each year by calling 751-4696. General Information 748-1623.

Chesterfield County Recreation Centers: The county operates no permanently located recreation centers. Park and recreation activities are held in various elementary schools throughout the county. The location of particular class or activity may vary from season. Call the Park and Recreation office (748-1623) or consult activities schedules available quarterly at library branches.

Chesterfield County Athletic Complexes:

> Bird Athletic Complex - south on Iron Bridge Road, left on Courthouse Road just past Bird High School. Picnic area, restrooms, lighted tennis courts and softball fields, basketball courts.
>
> Courthouse Athletic Complex - at the County Fairground behind the County Administration buildings on Iron Bridge Road. Picnic and play areas, lighted softball and football fields, restrooms. Also rental facilities for equestrian events. See Horseback Riding.
>
> Greenfield Athletic Complex - at Greenfield Elementary School on Greenfield Road off Robious Road east of Huguenot Road. Play equipment, softball and soccer fields.
>
> Monacan Athletic Complex - adjacent to Monacan High School, Smoketree Dr. off Courthouse Road south of Route 60. Picnic tables, softball and soccer fields.
>
> Providence Athletic Complex - at Providence Middle School, Providence Road just south of Route 60. Tennis courts, softball, football and soccer fields.
>
> Robious Athletic Complex - west on Huguenot Road, right on Robious, first right on Robious Crossing Drive, behind

elementary school. Picnic tables, playground, tennis and basketball courts, softball, football, soccer fields, concessions and restrooms.

Libraries

Most branches in Richmond, Henrico, Chesterfield and Goochland systems have free, weekly story hours and films for preschoolers, and some have these programs for toddlers as well. There are craft activities and after school films for older children. Sometimes the evening films for adults are also of interest to children.

When school lets out in June, the summer reading and listening clubs begin.

City and county residents are allowed to have cards at both Richmond and Henrico or Chesterfield libraries at no charge.

Hours vary considerably from branch to branch. Some stay open until 9pm every weekday except Friday. Many have evening hours on specific nights only or close their children's section early.

Chesterfield County

Central Library, 9501 Lori Road 751-4955
Bon Air, 9103 Rattlesnake Road 320-2461
Chester, 12140 Harrowgate Road 748-6314
Clover Hill, 6701 Deer Run Drive 739-7335.
Enon, 1801 Enon Church Road 530-3403;
Ettrick-Matoaca, 4501 River Road 526-8087
La Prade, 2730 Hicks Road, 276-7755
Meadowdale, 4301 Meadowdale Blvd. 743-4842,
Midlothian, 521 Coalfield Road 794-7907
Outreach Services 748-1768

Goochland County

Goochland Library 556-4774

Henrico County The Henrico County Library system features a collection of almost 700,000 volumes. A variety of programming for juveniles is provided and a bookmobile serves patrons without ready access to a library.

The "Answer Line" is for general information, book availability and reference services. Dial 222-1318.

> Business Resource Center, 4060 Innslake Drive 747-0156
> Dumbarton, Staples Mill and Penick Roads 262-6507
> Fairfield, 1001 North Laburnum Avenue 222-1559
> Gayton, 10600 Gayton Road 740-2747
> Glen Allen, 10501 Staples Mill Road 756-7523
> Innsbrook, 4060 Innslake Drive 747-8140
> North Park, Parham Road and Route 1, 262-4876
> Sandston, 23 East Williamsburg Road 737-3728
> Tuckahoe, 1700 Parham Road 270-9578
> Varina, 2001 Library Road 222-3414
> County municipal library (municipal reference and law library), Hungary Spring and Parham Roads at the Henrico County Courthouse 672-4780

Richmond

> Main Library, 101 East Franklin Street 780-4672
> Belmont, 3100 Ellwood Avenue 780-6139
> Bon Air, 9103 Rattlesnake Road 320-2461
> Broad Rock, 4820 Warwick Road 780-5072
> East End, 2414 "R" Street 780-4474
> Ginter Park, 1200 Westbrook Avenue 780-6236
> Hull Street, 1400 Hull Street 780-5080
> North Avenue, 2901 North Avenue 321-7985

West End, 5420 Patterson Avenue 285-8820

Westover Hills, 1408 Westover Hills Boulevard 780-5055

Pamunkey Regional Library serves the counties of Hanover, Goochland, King William and King and Queen as well as the towns of Ashland and West Point. There are eight branch libraries with daily delivery among the libraries and a bookmobile linked by a computer system. The library features a good collection of books, magazines, talking books and videos, and special children's programs.

Hanover County

Ashland Branch Library, 102 South Railroad Avenue 798-4072, open 10am-9pm Monday-Thursday; 10am-6pm Friday and Saturday.

Hanover Branch Library, 7527 Library Drive, U.S. Route 301, 537-6210 or 730-6210, 9am-9pm Monday-Wednesday; 9am-6pm Thursday and Friday; 9am-2pm Saturday.

Mechanicsville Branch Library, 7179 Stonewall Parkway 746-9615, 10am-9pm Monday-Thursday; 10am-6pm Friday and Saturday.

Rockville Branch Library, 16600 Pouncey Tract Road 749-3146, 1-9pm Monday-Tuesday; 10am-9pm Wednesday and Thursday; 10am-6pm Friday and Saturday.

The Bookmobile serves the Hanover area on Tuesdays and Thursdays at different locations alternately.

Recreational Opportunities for the Handicapped

(All parks have adaptations for wheelchair access. See individual park listings.)

Camp Baker 7600 Beach Road, Chesterfield County 748-4789. Year-round respite care and summer camp for mentally retarded children and adults, ages 6 and up. Swimming, arts and crafts, nature trails, music and dances. Fees based on ability to pay.

Chimborazo Park Parcourse Fitness Cluster designed especially for use by disabled residents. For more information, see Parks, Chimborazo.

Easter Seal Society of Virginia 9291 Laurel Grove Road, Mechanicsville 746-1007. Year-round camping and recreation programs for children and adults and their families. Weekend retreats and summer camps in the mountains and in Caroline County. Arts and crafts, nature study, canoeing, music, dance, drama, horseback riding, tent camping.

Iron Bridge Park Route 10, Chesterfield County. ¼-mile paved trail with exercise equipment adapted for use by the handicapped. See Parks, Iron Bridge.

Parent-to-Parent Program 1518 Willow Lawn Drive 282-4255. Network for parents of handicapped/disabled children. Call for brochure on recreational resources plus other information on community, educational and personal resources.

School of the Performing Arts in the Richmond Community (SPARC) 1205 West Main Street 355-2662. SPARC offers special classes for the hearing impaired. Call for more information.

St. Joseph's Villa 8000 Brook Road 266-2447. Weekend and after school care and recreational programs for mentally retarded children and adults, ages 2-21, plus summer program.

Youth Ballet Program City of Richmond sponsors a ballet program for the visually or hearing impaired. See Chapter 6, Arts Instruction, Dance.

Summer Camps

The following list provides a brief outline of the many camps and activities available to children during the summer months. This listing is by no means complete but attempts to offer examples of the many different camps available in the Richmond and surrounding areas. Contact individual organizations for more information.

Camp Hanover Mechanicsville 779-2811. This Christian ministry offers traditional adventure and family activities in a rustic setting. Ages 4th-12th grade.

Camp Hilbert Goochland 288-6091. Horseback riding, archery, canoeing, hiking, swimming and more are offered at this 111-acre expanse operated by the Jewish Community Center. Some summer activities also take place at 5403 Monument Avenue (288-6091). Ages K-10th grade.

Camp T. Brady Saunders Goochland 355-4306. This Boy Scout camp of the Robert E. Lee Council features rappelling, sailing and opportunities to earn merit badges.

Camp Thunderbird Outdoor Center Chesterfield 748-6714. Boys and girls ages 5-16 can swim, hike, boat, fish and much more in this day camp.

St. Catherine's Creative Arts Program (CAT'S CAP) 6001 Grove Avenue 288-2804. This program offers 2nd through 8th graders more than 140 different classes in various arts-related areas. Dance, film, theater, sports, survival skills, computers and more are offered in half-day and full-day classes.

A "Young Explorers Program" is also offered for children ages 3½-1st grade and runs concurrently with the older program for half-day sessions only.

Chesterfield County Parks and Recreation 748-1623. Summer history camps, Rockwood nature camps and Camp Chesterfield mean a summer filled with fun and activities for children ages 6-12.

City Slickers Summer Camp 788-4949. Three of Richmond's top child-related organizations have put together this exceptional summer program. The Maymont Foundation, the Richmond Children's Museum and the Valentine Museum provide quality education at Maymont for 7-12 year olds. Classes are limited in size. 6-week sessions include art, "City Slicker Sleuths," river week, nature explorers, theater, etc. Camps run from July through mid-August.

Collegiate School 741-9714. Offers a wide variety of camps for children ages 3-12. Horizons Unlimited concentrates on theater, adventure, arts and archaeology while Young Cubs, Explorer Cubs and other "Cubs" programs begin in mid-June and run into August.

A Summer Academic Institute is also offered for ages 9th grade-adult, which includes theater, computers, college board reviews, courses for credit, etc.

Commonwealth Girl Scout Council of Virginia 7300 Hanover Green Drive 746-0590. Girls ages 6-17 can take part in numerous Day Camp and Resident Camp activities even if not girl scouts. 4-, 6-, 11-, and 23-day programs are available.

Challenge Discovery Outdoor Adventures Richmond 639-1544. Outdoor adventure programs with emphasis on "adventure," with girls and boys grades 5-8 able to climb rocks, canoe, kayak, and white water paddle among other events.

Green Mornings Nature Camp Lewis Ginter Botanical Gardens, 1880 Lakeside Avenue 262-9887. What better place to have fun and learn about nature and the world of plants? Programs are aimed at rising 2nd-5th graders.

Also available is the unique Mountain Mania Nature Camp for 6-8th graders interested in a trip to the mountains, complete with camping out under a starry sky.

Hand Workshop Art Center 1812 West Main Street 353-0094. For 15 years the Hand Workshop's Teaching New Talent program has offered 8-18 year olds the opportunity to work with a professional artist to learn new skills. 72 morning and afternoon courses are offered in pottery, video animation, drawing, stained glass and much more.

Hanover County Parks & Recreation 798-8062. Supervised recreational activities are offered each summer throughout the county. These Youth Summer Day Camps are for kids K-middle school. They last approximately 7 weeks and offer many varied activities and themes.

Henrico County Parks & Recreation 672-4198. Camp Henrico begins in June for children ages 8-15 and runs through mid-August, offering various arts and crafts programs, fishing, cooking, hiking and field trips. Also, a summer playgrounds program runs from the end of June into August.

JCC's Sports Camp 5403 Monument Avenue 288-6091. Children in grades 1-8 can enjoy baseball, roller hockey, basketball, gymnastics and other sports at the Sports Zone, located at the Jewish Community Center. Preschoolers won't be left out, thanks to Camp Ganim's arts and crafts and more in the World of Discovery Preschool Camp.

Luther Memorial School 321-6420. This school's weekly day camps are theme-oriented with each week devoted to swimming, art, sports and other activities for children from the age of 3 through 1st grade. This program runs for 10 weeks.

Second through fourth graders may participate in the "Junior Arts in the Summer" program where sports, drama and arts are emphasized. 5th-9th graders are eligible for the "Arts in the Summer" program which has similar themes, with the addition of computers, etc.

Maymont Summer Discovery Camp 1700 Hampton Street 358-7166. Nature is explored in all of its many forms in Maymont's camp for children 4½ to 13. Camps run from mid-June through mid-August. New for 1997 was the Environmental Adventures camp for ages 9-13. This camp is designed for preteens with a fascination for science.

Appendix

Montessori Child Care at the Arboretum 323-6229. Children ages 6-8 enjoy gymnastics, sports, computers and more from mid-June through mid-August.

Museum of the Confederacy's Civil War Summer Camps 1201 East Clay 649-1861. Explore Civil War history through the Civil War day camps, beginning in late June and running through early August. These are week-long day camps running 9am-4pm each day. Exploring Civil War history at the museum and around Richmond is the order of the day for 4th through 9th graders.

Richmond City Department of Parks, Recreation and Community Facilities 780-6091. Ready for Summer programs are offered at 23 neighborhood recreational centers and playgrounds around the city. Also featured are special Saturday Nature Programs at the James River Park.

Richmond Montessori School 741-0040. Children ages 3-13 take part in drama, arts, poetry, creative writing and more in three sessions beginning in July.

The Sabot School 6818 West Grace Street 288-4122. The Sabot School offers several week-long summer day camps for ages 3-10. These half-day sessions change themes each week and may include beach week, exploring space, dinosaur week, nature and animals. Age appropriate themes and fun are emphasized, while Sabot's philosophy of "Play is learning and Learning is play" is practiced throughout the sessions.

Science Museum of Virginia 2500 West Broad Street 367-6552. Future scientists will thrive in the museum's summer programs for children ages 4 through 12 with the Science Explorers, Junior Science Explorers and Senior Science Explorers.

St. Christopher's School 282-3185. Science, computer, multimedia, sports and more for children from 2nd grade through 8th grade.

Stony Point School 272-1341. 28 acres of nature and wildlife provide the setting for a summer of adventure at the Stony Point School. Three

2-week sessions beginning in late June. Nature learning stations are just one of the unique features of this summer program for children ages 5-12.

Virginia Museum of Fine Arts 2800 Grove Avenue 367-0844. Workshops and classes are offered at the museum in their Art Venture and Short Takes Workshops.

YMCA 2 West Franklin Street 649-9622. Weekly programs for kids can be found at all Richmond-area YMCAs. Camp Thunderbird is for children ages 5-16 in Chesterfield County and offers outdoor activities such as boating, fishing, hiking and archery.

Parenting Centers

Commonwealth Parenting Center 8002 Discovery Drive 289-4990. Resource center for parents and teachers providing workshops, support groups, and individual consultation by counselors specializing in early childhood and adolescent development. Referral service for child care, as well as mental health care, diagnostic and tutorial services, educational assessment and teacher training programs.

Memorial Guidance Clinic 2319 East Broad Street 649-1605. Provides counseling for emotionally disturbed children, child care resources and referral (KID CARE), and educational materials and workshops for parents, teachers and others interested in strengthening the family.

"Kid Talk," a telephone "warmline" for advice on child-rearing (649-0218), provides parents with an easy source of information and support on child development and behavior.

Parent-to-Parent Program 1518 Willow Lawn Drive 282-4255. Counseling resource center for parents and children. Also offers services to handicapped children.

Parents and Children Coping Together, Inc. 306 West Broad Street 225-0002. Counseling for emotionally disturbed children and adolescents and their parents.

Index

A

Airports 144
Amusement Parks 141-142
Art Supplies 158-160
Arts & Crafts Studios 145
Arts Instruction 110-115
    Dance 113-115
    Music 112
    Theater 110-111

B

Banking 146
Blue Ridge Parkway 138
B'nai B'rith 174
Bookstores 156-158
Boy Scouts of America 174
Boys & Girls Clubs 174

C

Calendars 5-6
Camps
    See Summer Camps
Cemeteries 21-22
Chesterfield County
    Athletic Complexes 179-180
    Camps 184
    Courthouse Complex 122
    Extension Agents 67
    Fire Department 151-152
    Hiking Trails 91
    Libraries 180
    Parks 52-56
    Parks and Recreation 84, 178-179, 184
    Police Dept. & Programs 151
    Team Sports 99, 101-102
Christmas Trees, cut-your-own 71-73
Churches 20-21
Circus 118
Civil War 4, 14-15, 17, 19-22, 24, 28-29, 38, 42-43, 47-48, 55, 80, 91, 128, 136, 171

Clothing, New 164-165
Clothing, Used 163-164
Community Centers 97-98, 176-182
Cruises 137-138

D

Dance Companies 109-110

E

Educational Supplies 158-160

F

Farmers Market 148
Farms 67-71, 146-147
Film 107
Fire Departments
    See County Listings
freshwater springs 66

G

General Information 2
Girl Scouts 174
Golf Courses 86-87
Goochland County
    Extension Agents 67
    Libraries 183
    Museum 13
    Newspaper 4
    Parade 119
Greenhouses 146-147

H

Hanover County
    Extension Agent 67
    Hiking Trails 89-90
    Libraries 182
    Newspaper 4
    Parks 48-49
    Parks and Recreation Dept. 99
    Summer Camp 186

Team Sports 100, 102
Henrico County
    Community Centers 178
    Extension Agent 67
    Fire Department 150-151
    Hiking Trails 90-91
    Libraries 181
    Parks 49-52
    Parks & Recreation Dept. 99, 177-178
    Police Department 150
    Summer Camps 186
    Team Sports 99, 102
Historic Homes 22-26
    Agecroft Hall 23-24
    Berkeley Plantation 24
    Centre Hill Mansion 24
    Edgewood Plantation 23
    Monticello 139-140
    Montpelier 139
    Scotchtown 23
    Sherwood Forest Plantation 23
    Shirley Plantation 25
    Tuckahoe Plantation 25
    Virginia House 25
    Washington's Birthplace 140
    Westover Plantation 23
    Wilton House Museum 26
Historic Sites
    Capitol Square 18
    Governor's Mansion 18
    Pioneer Farmstead 18
    Richmond National Battlefield Park 19
    Virginia State Capitol 19
    Virginia War Memorial 20
Hobby Shops 162-163
Horse shows 119, 121

I

Information Centers
    Bell Tower-Capitol Square 7
    Metro-Richmond/Travelland 6
    Richmond International Airport 7
    Statewide Visitor Centers 7
Internet Web Sites 168-172
    Colleges and Universities 169
    Education Resources 171-172
    Local and State Interest 168
    Museums 170-171
    Newspapers and Magazines 170
    Public Radio and TV 169

J

James River Park System 45-48, 82-84, 89
Jewish Community Center 98, 174

K

Kanawha Canal 39-40

L

Libraries 17, 180-182

M

Maps 5
Markets, Food 148
Media (tours) 148
    Richmond Newspapers 148
    WCVE Channel 23 Public Television 149
    WRVA Talk Radio 149
    WRVQ/Q94 149
    WWBT Channel 12 Television 149
Monument Avenue 26-29
Monuments 26-31
Movie Theaters 107
Museums 10-18, 26, 128, 132-138
    American Historical Fnd. Museum 11
    Black History Museum/Cultural Ctr. 11
    Casemate Museum 136
    Chesterfield County Museum 11-12
    Children's Museum of Richmond 10
    Cong. Beth Ahabah Museum 12
    Elegba Folklore Society Cultural Ctr 12
    Goddard Space Flight Center 135
    Goochland Co. Historical Center 13
    Magnolia Grange Museum 13
    Mariners Museum 136
    John Marshall House 13-14
    Meadow Farm Museum 14
    Money Museum 14

Index

Museum Reference Library 17
Old Dominion Railway Museum 15
Petersburg Siege Museum 128
Edgar Allan Poe Museum 12
Portsmouth Museums 134
Virginia Randolph Memorial 15
U.S. Army Transportation 132
U.S. Slo-Pitch Softball Hall of Fame 128
Valentine Museum 16
Virginia Air and Space Center 136
Virginia Aviation Museum 16
Virginia Discovery Museum 138
Virginia Fire & Police Museum 12-13
Virginia Historical Society 17-18
Virginia Living Museum 136-137
Virginia Marine Science Museum 135
Virginia Museum of Fine Arts 16-17
Virginia Telephone Museum 18
Maggie L. Walker House 13
Watermen's Museum 132
White House of the Confederacy 15
Music Series
    Carpenter Center 108
    Classic Amphitheatre at Strawberry Hill 109
    Community Bands & Choruses 109
    Landmark Theater 109
    Musical Mondays at Maymont 108
    Richmond Classical Players 108
    Richmond Coliseum 109
    Richmond Philharmonic 108
    Richmond Symphony 108
    Virginia Museum of Fine Arts 108
    Virginia Opera 108
    Wolf Trap Farm Park 140-141

N

National Weather Service 8, 153
Neighboring Areas
    Central Virginia 128-129
    Historic Triangle 129-132
    Jamestown 131-132
    Mountains 138-140
    Northern Neck 140
    Petersburg 128
    Tidewater 133-138
    Washington, DC 140-141
    Williamsburg 129-130, 141
Nuclear Power Stations 152

O

Outdoor Concerts 116-117

P

Parenting Centers 188-189
Parks
    See County Listings
Pick-Your-Own Farms 67-71
Plantations
    See Historic Homes
Police Departments
    See County Listings
Prepaid Education Program 169
Publications
    Falls of the James Atlas 40
    Going Places With Children (in DC) 140
    Guide to Historic Virginia 4
    Guide to the Works of the James River and Kanawha Co. 40
    Guide to Virginia's Civil War 4
    Innsbrook Today 3
    Insider's Guide to Greater Richmond 4
    Metropolitan Richmond Visitor's Guide 4
    Neighborhood newspapers 4
    Newspapers & Magazines on the Internet 170
    Parks, Preserves and Rivers: A Guidebook 5
    Richmond Magazine 3
    Richmond Parents Monthly Magz. 3
    Richmond Times-Dispatch 3, 148
    Shenandoah Overlook 138
    Style Weekly 3, 170
    Virginia Family Adventure Guide 5
    Virginia Outdoor Activity Guide, 5
    Virginia Travel Guide 5
    Zoopack: The Teacher's Guide to the Virginia Zoological Park 133

Richmond Is for Children

R

Recorded Telephone Messages
    Adventure Fun Line 8
    Children's Museum of Richmond 7
    Classic Amphitheatre at Strawberry Hill 7
    Innsbrook After Hours 7
    National Weather Service 8
    Richmond Coliseum 7
    Richmond Ski Club Fun Line 8
    Science Museum of Virginia 8
    Ski reports 96
    Skywatch Information (weather) 8
    Time and Temperature 8
    Time of Day 8
    WWBT Call 12 line 8
    XL102/Q94 Info Line 7
Recreation Centers & Organizations 174-180
Recreational Opportunities for the Handicapped 182-183
Richmond, City of
    Convention & Visitors Bureau 4
    Fire Department 151
    James River Park System 45-48, 89
    Parks 34-48
    Parks and Recreation Dept. 99, 105
    Police Department 151
Ringling Bros. Circus 118

S

Salvation Army Boys & Girls Club 175
Science Centers
    Lewis Ginter Botanical Garden at Bloemendaal 65
    Lora Robins Gallery of Design from Nature 64-65
    Science Museum of Virginia 64
Scientific Places of Interest
    Metro Richmond Zoo 66
    Morefield Mines 66
    Springs, freshwater 66
Seasonal Events 117-125
Skyline Drive 138

Sports, Participatory
    Bicycling 79-81
    Boating, Tubing 82-83
    Bowling 81-82
    Camping 84
    Canoeing 83-84
    Fishing 84-86
    Golf 86-87
    Gymnastics 87-88
    Hiking 88-91
    Horseback Riding 91-93
    Ice-Skating and Sledding 93-94
    Marathons 94
    Roller-Skating 94-95
    Skiing 96
    Swimming 96-98
    Tennis 102
Sports, Spectator 76-79
    Auto racing 77-78
    Nations Bank City Tennis Championships 79
    Nike Dominion Open, Golf 78
    Nuveen Tour, Tennis 79
    Richmond Braves Baseball 76
    Richmond Coliseum 76
    Richmond Dragway 77
    Richmond Intl. Raceway 77
    Richmond Kickers Soccer 78
    Richmond Renegades Ice Hockey 78
    Southside Speedway 77
    Virginia Motorsports Park 77-78
Sports, Spectator (college) 76-77
    Randolph-Macon College 77
    University of Richmond 76
    Virginia Commonwealth University 76
    Virginia State University 77
    Virginia Union University 77
Sports, Team 99-102
    Challenger baseball 100
    Little League 99-101
    Soccer 101-102
    Softball 99-101
State Parks and Preserves 56-59
    Bear Creek Lake State Park 57
        See Boat Rentals
    Chippokes Plantation State Park 57

Index

    False Cape State Park 134
    Holliday Lake State Park 58
    Lake Anna State Park 58
    Pocahontas State Park and State
        Forest 58-59
    Twin Lakes State Park 59
    York River State Park 59
Summer Camps 184-188

T

Telephone Messages
  See Recorded Telephone Messages
Television 6
Theater 104-107
Ticketmaster 7
Toys 160-162

U

U.S. Secret Service 152
Utilities 152-153

W

Washington, D.C. 140-141
Water Treatment Facility 153
Weather Forecasting & Reporting 153
Websites
    See Internet Web Sites
Wildlife Preserves 60-61, 134

Y

YMCAs 98, 175, 188
YWCA 98, 175

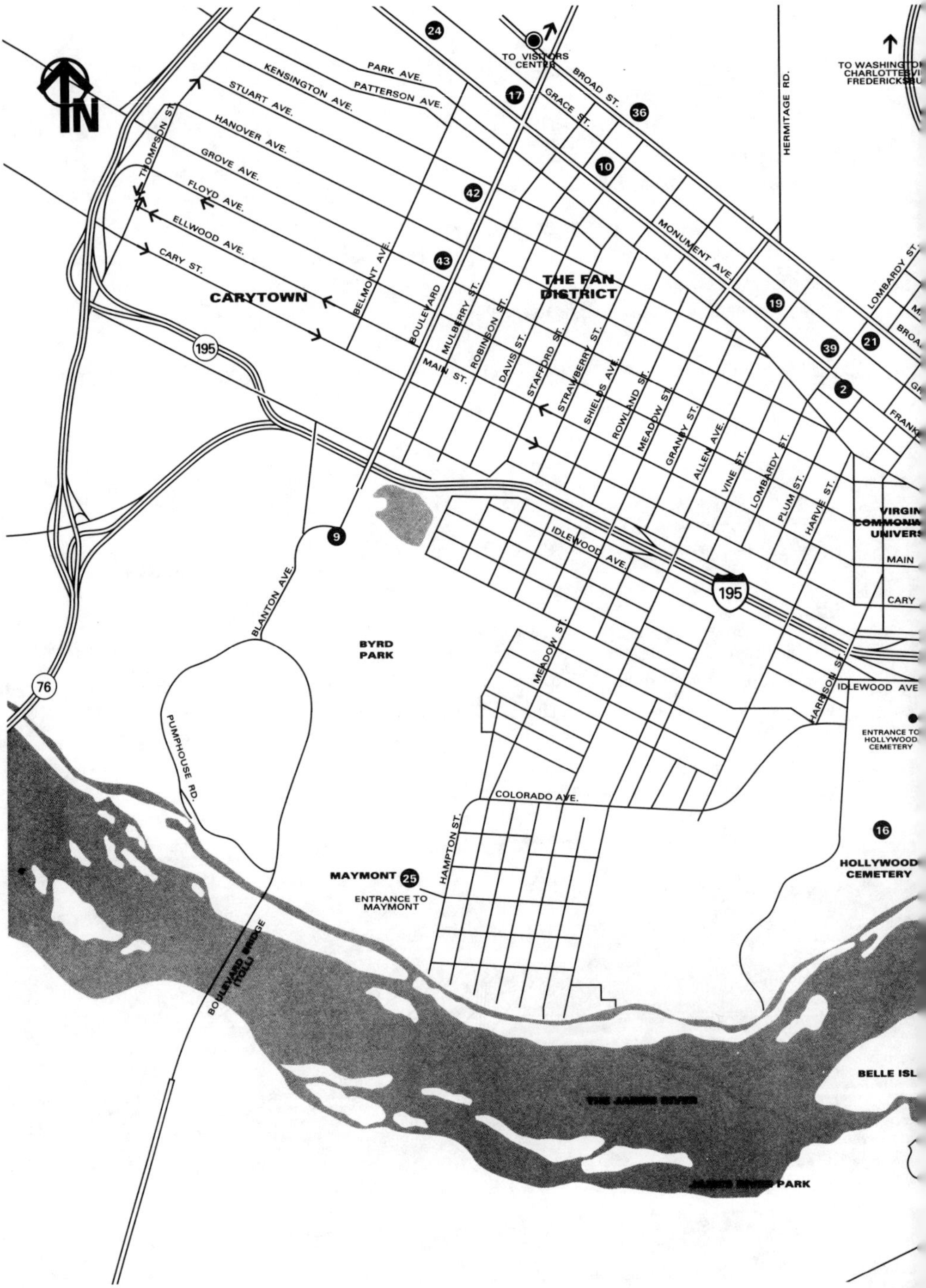
N
TO VISITORS CENTRE
PARK AVE.
KENSINGTON AVE.
PATTERSON AVE.
STUART AVE.
HANOVER AVE.
GROVE AVE.
FLOYD AVE.
ELLWOOD AVE.
CARY ST.
THOMPSON ST.
BROAD ST.
GRACE ST.
HERMITAGE RD.
MONUMENT AVE.
CARYTOWN
THE FAN DISTRICT
BELMONT AVE.
BOULEVARD
MULBERRY ST.
ROBINSON ST.
DAVIS ST.
STAFFORD ST.
STRAWBERRY ST.
SHIELDS AVE.
ROWLAND ST.
MEADOW ST.
GRANBY ST.
ALLEN AVE.
VINE ST.
LOMBARDY ST.
PLUM ST.
HARVIE ST.
MAIN ST.
IDLEWOOD AVE.
MAIN
CARY
195
76
BLANTON AVE.
BYRD PARK
PUMPHOUSE RD.
HARRISON ST.
ENTRANCE TO HOLLYWOOD CEMETERY
HOLLYWOOD CEMETERY
COLORADO AVE.
HAMPTON ST.
MAYMONT
ENTRANCE TO MAYMONT
BOULEVARD BRIDGE (TOLL)
BELLE ISL
24
17
36
10
42
43
19
21
39
2
9
25
16

Downtown Richmond, Virginia

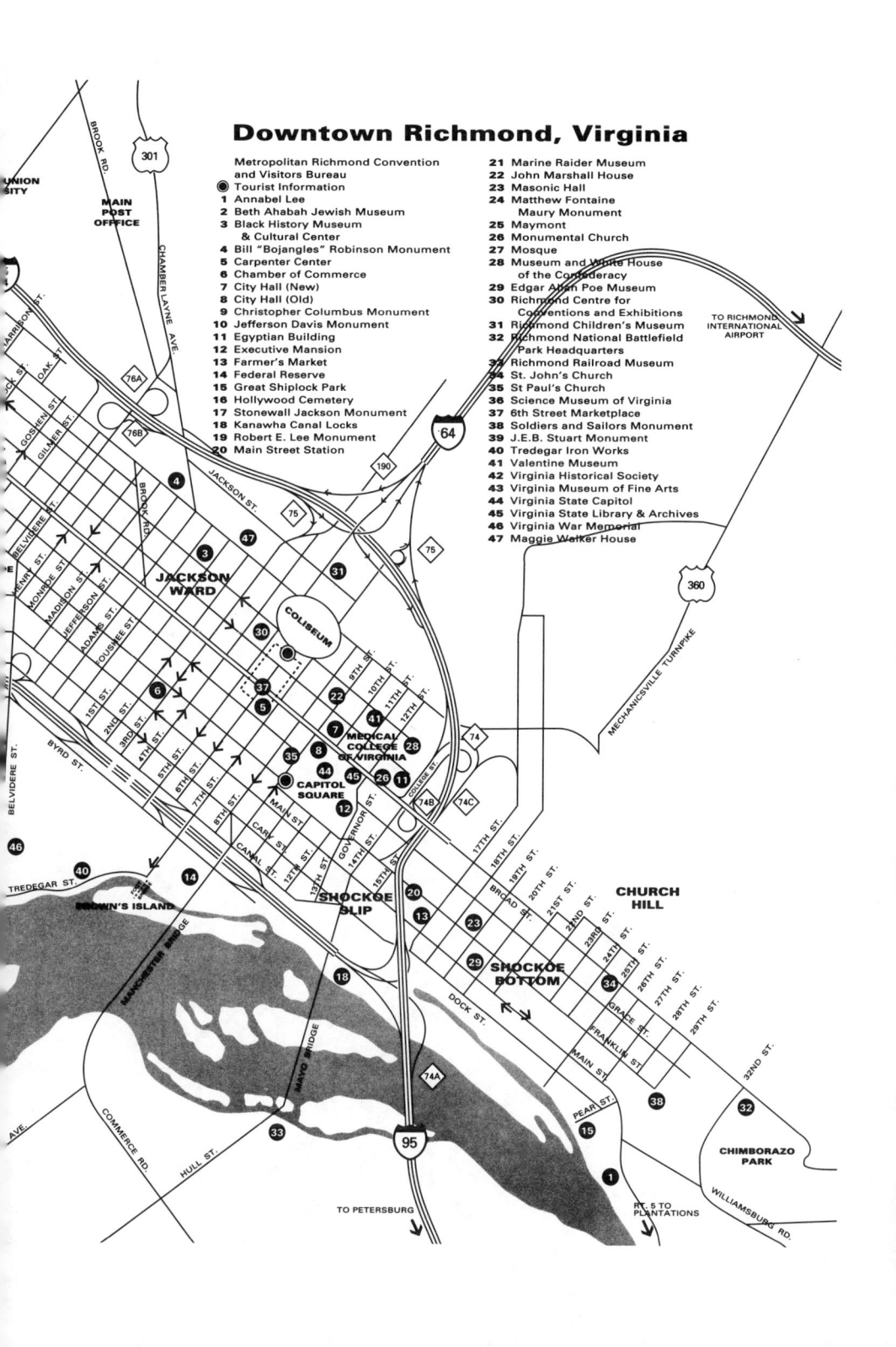

- Metropolitan Richmond Convention and Visitors Bureau
- ⊙ Tourist Information
1. Annabel Lee
2. Beth Ahabah Jewish Museum
3. Black History Museum & Cultural Center
4. Bill "Bojangles" Robinson Monument
5. Carpenter Center
6. Chamber of Commerce
7. City Hall (New)
8. City Hall (Old)
9. Christopher Columbus Monument
10. Jefferson Davis Monument
11. Egyptian Building
12. Executive Mansion
13. Farmer's Market
14. Federal Reserve
15. Great Shiplock Park
16. Hollywood Cemetery
17. Stonewall Jackson Monument
18. Kanawha Canal Locks
19. Robert E. Lee Monument
20. Main Street Station
21. Marine Raider Museum
22. John Marshall House
23. Masonic Hall
24. Matthew Fontaine Maury Monument
25. Maymont
26. Monumental Church
27. Mosque
28. Museum and White House of the Confederacy
29. Edgar Allan Poe Museum
30. Richmond Centre for Conventions and Exhibitions
31. Richmond Children's Museum
32. Richmond National Battlefield Park Headquarters
33. Richmond Railroad Museum
34. St. John's Church
35. St Paul's Church
36. Science Museum of Virginia
37. 6th Street Marketplace
38. Soldiers and Sailors Monument
39. J.E.B. Stuart Monument
40. Tredegar Iron Works
41. Valentine Museum
42. Virginia Historical Society
43. Virginia Museum of Fine Arts
44. Virginia State Capitol
45. Virginia State Library & Archives
46. Virginia War Memorial
47. Maggie Walker House